ALONG
AN INNER
SHORE

With the coming of evening Jesus said to his disciples, 'Let us cross over to the far shore of the lake.'

So they put to sea. As they sailed a storm broke over the lake, so violent that the waves were breaking into the boat.

But he was in the stern, his head on the cushion, asleep.

They woke him and said to him: 'Master! Master! Do you not care? We are going down!'

He rose, rebuked the wind, and said to the sea, 'Hush! Be still!' The wind dropped, and there was a dead calm.

He said to them, 'Why are you so frightened? How is it that you have no faith?

Matthew 8.18, 23–27; Mark 4.35–41;
Luke 8.22–25.

ALONG AN INNER SHORE

Echoes from the Gospel

by

Brother Leonard of Taizé

The Pilgrim Press
New York

First published 1986
by A. R. Mowbray & Co. Ltd,
Saint Thomas House, Becket Street,
Oxford, OX1 1SJ

Library of Congress Cataloging in Publication Data
Leonard, of Taizé, Brother, 1940–
   Along an inner shore.
   1. Meditations.   I. Title.
BV4832.2.L455   1986   242   86–4892
ISBN 0–8298–0733–0 (pbk.)

The Pilgrim Press, 132 West 31 Street, New York, NY 10001

Printed and bound in Great Britain

ACKNOWLEDGEMENTS
Extracts from 'The Return' and 'The Transfiguration' are reprinted by permission of Faber and Faber Limited from *The Collected Poems of Edwin Muir*.
An extract from *The Everlasting Man* by G.K. Chesterton is reproduced by permission of Burns & Oates Ltd.
All Scripture quotations in this publication are from the Holy Bible, New International Version. Copyright © 1973, 1978, 1984, International Bible Society.
Excerpt from *The Habit of Being* by Flannery O'Connor Copyright © 1979 by Regina O'Connor. Reprinted by permission of Farrar, Straus and Giroux, Inc.

To my sisters and my brother

AUTHOR'S NOTE
AND ACKNOWLEDGEMENTS

This book was written at Taizé, France, during the summer of 1985. Taizé is the village in Burgundy where Brother Roger founded in 1940 an ecumenical monastic community which is now made up of eighty Catholic and Protestant brothers from some twenty different countries. Through their life together, the brothers of Taizé attempt to be a parable of community and of reconciliation. Taizé is also a place of welcome. Starting in the 1960s, several successive generations of young adults from the whole of Europe as well as other continents, have come to Taizé in ever increasing numbers, exploring the sources of faith.

Most of the brothers live at Taizé, others in small communities among the poor in different parts of the world: in Africa, Asia, North and South America. Over the past years I have been part of the small Taizé community in Hell's Kitchen, on 48th Street, in Manhattan. Besides our presence in the neighbourhood and in the city, the New York brothers have been involved in a 'pilgrimage of reconciliation' throughout the United States and Canada. My two previous books, *Listening to People of Hope** and *Belonging**, grew out of my life in New York and of my involvement with the other brothers in this pilgrimage.

The original invitation to write brief meditations for daily use throughout a whole year came from Marion M. Meyer, senior editor at The Pilgrim Press, New York. But the book changed its shape in the process of being written.

Beyond the inner circle of the Community of Taizé, some friends passing through Taizé during the summer of 1985 saw part of the book as it evolved, and in turn enriched its contents: Jon James (on the way back from the Holy Land to Hawaii), Pamela Meidell and Marie Milis (travelling together through Europe), Lydia and Craig Holley (just settled in Europe). With each of them the conversation went far beyond the actual texts we read together. With each of them I found myself walking on the road to Emmaeus, listening and wondering.

At the end of the summer I took the book with me to New York and let it rest there while pursuing with other brothers of Taizé our 'pilgrimage of reconciliation' around the US. During that time Sister Mary-Christine Morkovsky, CPD (Ogdensburg, NY) read the entire typescript. Back in New York I felt ready to send the book into the world!

Finally, it is a joy for me to have a picture of one of my own mother's oil paintings on the cover of this book. Would she ever have imagined this?

New York, All Souls 1985

** Published by Mowbray, London and Oxford, and by The Pilgrim Press, New York.*

CONTENTS

Introduction

This book of meditations begins at Easter and travels back to Christmas. Both events stand at either extremity of the mystery of Christ, but Easter celebrates the living Christ welcoming us today. Easter is the dawn of humanity. It is Easter every morning. Easter stands at the beginning of our forgiven existence. It is the headline, the prototype and the testament of my own life. From Easter I look back upon the Passion, the journeys and encounters in Jesus' ministry, and finally upon Christmas. And at Christmas, as though encountering a *da capo* at the end of the line, I am sent back to Easter again.

This retrospective movement from Easter (1) to the Passion (2), the Ministry (3) and to Christmas (4) is retraced in each of the four chapters of this book in fourteen stations of life. Texts from the Gospel guide each station, but I have been able to impart only a glimpse of their lustre in each one of the meditations. In preparing this book, I have been impressed as never before by the purity and the transcendence of the Gospel. These echoes from the Gospel are therefore no more than the wheat, waving in the wind, as compared to the radiance of the sunlight, the blowing wind and the full harvest of the Gospel.

While travelling in the Gospel I have found myself often on the way to Emmaeus, walking behind two disciples involved in a lively discussion with a Stranger. I have tried to catch scraps of the conversation. Unfortunately, unable to remain all the time in their footsteps, distracted and distraught, I haven't heard everything, especially not the beginning with all the references to Moses and the prophets. At times I have been simply struck with awe by this Stranger 'given up into the power of human beings', standing there with uplifted hands. I felt my heart on fire when the Stranger invited me, too, to enter into his home, when he broke the bread and offered it to me. At that moment I saw, in the twinkling of an eye, that 'death is swallowed up in victory.'

Life is a labyrinth, a labyrinth of longing, but, again and again, I encountered this Stranger tenderly enlightening my path. So I travelled retrospectively in the Gospel, recalling how he had welcomed us from the source of his being in Golgotha's garden on the mount of the transfiguration and walking on the water, how he had descended into suffering and death and drunk the cup of human distress, how he had journeyed in Galilee, that obscure province of the Roman Empire, as a light to whom people entrusted themselves, how he, in a brief tenderness, had illumined the long and dark history of humanity by his birth in a manger and by Mary's embrace while the donkey ran, in no time, all the way to Egypt.

I have never thought about him as only belonging to the past. Times coincide in him, cultures unite, the past runs towards its future, all human history finds its transcendence in Christ, the Living One. And ever since he vanished from my sight at Emmaeus, I have been ceaselessly searching for him along an inner shore.

1

Christ welcomes you with such joy

But he will come again, it's said, though not
Unwanted and unsummoned. . . . In our own time,
Some say, or at a time when time is ripe.
Then he will come, Christ the uncrucified,
Christ the discrucified, his death undone,
His agony unmade, his cross dismantled –
Glad to be so – and the tormented wood
Will cure its hurt and grow into a tree
In a green springing corner of young Eden.

– Edwin Muir, *The Transfiguration*

(1) Home on Apple Blossom Day

> 'Rabbi' (which means Teacher), 'where are you staying?'
> 'Come,' he replied, 'and you will see.'
>
> *John 1.38–39*

All the sugar maples in Canterbury, New Hampshire, have names. They are named after the homeless children this Shaker community used to take in. One sublime tree is named after Bertha, whom I met on her eighty-eighth birthday, in the Good Room next to an orchard where the apples lay in beds of mint. She is one of the last surviving Shakers. Both of her parents died when she was only four. Her sister took care of her for a few years, but when she wanted to marry, looking after her little sister became too much of a burden, and Bertha was placed in the Shaker village.

She has never forgotten that moment, on the top of the hill, as she watched her older sister's carriage go down the road and disappear. A Shaker girl saw her distress and led her down to the farm to show her the puppies, lambs and piglets. 'Don't cry', she said, 'we will take care of you.' She couldn't eat that evening; her sorrow was too great.

On the following Sunday the sound of a bell awakened her. Looking out of her window, she saw the Shakers gathering together. A young sister came into her room and said: 'Bertha, today is a special day, Apple Blossom Day. When the apple trees are at the peak of bloom, all the brothers, sisters and little children visit our five apple orchards and give praise and thanks to God.' Bertha ran out and got in line with the others. Soon the signal was given, and the line started moving across the meeting house field. It was a balmy day, the sky was azure blue, the fragrance of apple blossoms permeated the air.

In the first orchard the Shakers formed a big circle. The Elder said to all the young people, 'Everyone close your eyes and listen.' The children could actually hear the breeze moving through the grass and the birds whistling and the bees going about their work. Then the Elder offered a prayer. He asked for God's blessings, not only for themselves, but for people of every religion, every nation, every race. Even at that age Bertha realized that the earth needed people who care for the whole world. When they had visited all the orchards, the children ran back up the hill, leading the others. Everyone was singing. Bertha paused. In the distance she could see the white houses and the open doors of the Shaker village. Here, she thought, is my home.

Today, all her friends are dead, and she is blind. In the Good Room, on her eighty-eighth birthday, I ventured to ask: 'And tomorrow . . . the future?' She paused, and then in a young voice full of joy she replied: 'Oh, death is just the opening of another door.'

(2) The Wave in The Stadium

> He looked up to heaven and with a deep sigh said to him, 'Ephphatha' (which means, 'Be opened!') At this, the man's ears were opened, his tongue was loosened and he began to speak plainly.
>
> *Mark 7.34–35*

Tonight is 'Nostalgia Night' for all baseball fans in New York. We will have to be at the stadium three hours before the game starts, take our general admission tickets, get a free Brooklyn Dodger hat, buy a horn of popcorn and rejoice in the crowd, waiting for the magic of the baseball rituals. Is it because of the nostalgia we anticipate tonight that at breakfast the brothers and I begin a long talk about our childhood?

A big shadow was cast upon my childhood by a speech impediment that emerged when I was four years old, towards the end of World War Two. Was my difficulty in speaking linked to the events of the war? Was it an atavism? Was it rooted in an insecurity in life and love? Nobody knew the answer. Even today I refuse to apply the clinical term of stuttering to that continual nightmare; even today that word alone brings back a feeling of shame and humiliation to me. But I certainly spoke with an extreme hesitation, learned all kinds of stratagems and subterfuges to avoid a letter or a word that was doomed to lead me ineluctably into complete disaster, and found refuge in silence. Most of the time I took revenge by being as brilliant as possible in other areas of expression: listening, singing and playing baseball. During my entire childhood and adolescence I struggled with the effects of my problem. Humiliated, not always directly by others, but in myself, by the very act of speaking, that is to say by the painful impression I supposedly made on others – how could I then relate to others without making them victims of my own insecurity and incapacity to accept myself? I was called to the front of the classroom to answer questions about an essay I had written concerning 'the history of the tea'. I couldn't utter a word and had to return to my seat, defeated at my thousandth Waterloo. How could the soul of a ten-year-old child handle that? The first quarter of my life was dominated by this feeling of oppression and suffocation. It was quite a schooling for me!

But there was another side to this lingering problem. Growing up became a liberating experience of opening out, of breathtaking breathing space, of falling in love with life. A youth in desperate straits has an advantage in that adulthood can only be better, and even be filled with jubilation. Having been schooled in the Bible before I learned to read, I knew that word 'Ephphatha' that Jesus had spoken; all my faith was concentrated in that single word, and it still is. Even ageing creates in me the hope of finding access to a constantly widening horizon; even death unmasks itself to me as a new birth.

No existential problem disappears completely; life goes up and down. But problems are transcended and can become a stimulus, a motor, a launching pad. Built up inside oneself by a concrete suffering, confirmed by others in one's worth and presence, discovered in its real roots that invite a radical commitment, life becomes a dance of joy. Today I have more future than in my youth when I stood powerlessly before narrow gates. Ageing, however, consists not only in opening up but also in embracing one's own childhood and youth, returning there with the lantern of peace and reconciling oneself. The poet Edwin Muir sees himself returning to the house of his own life: 'I see myself sometimes, an old old man / . . . And I return / So altered, so adopted, to the house / Of my own life. / . . . And yet I cannot enter, for all within / Rises before me there, rises against me, / A sweet and terrible labyrinth of longing, / So that I turn aside and take the road / That always, early or late, runs on before.' But Jesus the Lord accompanies us in our inner adventure, in this inward pilgrimage to the fullness of life.

'How 'bout some noise?' flashes the screen on the

baseball field. Immediately people in the first section on the fourth level of the stadium stand up, lift up their arms, yell and sit down before the second section does the same. I have been thinking and thinking all day, immersed in my youth. But now this wave running through the crowd is like an image, a celebration of what my life is meant to be: a crossing over from confinement into the wide open.

(3) Cooking With a Blindfold

> 'A man was going down from Jerusalem to Jericho, when he fell into the hands of robbers. They stripped him of his clothes, beat him and went away, leaving him half dead . . . But a Samaritan, when he saw him, took pity on him. He went to him and bandaged his wounds, pouring on oil and wine.'
>
> *Luke 10.30, 33, 34*

When he was eight years old, one of the nuns at school caught him playing on the girls' side of the playground. As a result, he was locked in a room which had no windows and doors, waiting for school to be over with. He cried and cried. Finally, the nun returned and brought him back to the classroom. The boy knew that he couldn't tell his mother about the incident, fearing that she would blame him like the nun. The nun had told everybody that she would put him in a dress and fix his hair. Walking home, he crawled into some bushes on the side of the road, and prayed, 'God, please help with this.' Finally he understood that there is no help, that he himself was the help.

The child has long since become a man, and many humiliations have followed the one in the classroom. But since the awful experience of the nun's punishment, he has learned three lessons in helping himself. First, he discovered that we all have sorrows. The second lesson he learned was that 'forgiveness offers all things'. And that as soon as you are okay, you should be helping other people, not out of a feeling of responsibility or guilt, but because it is your pleasure to do so.

Some years ago, this man – he works as a cook – started to feel afraid to undertake things. Although he had never been afraid of flying, suddenly he was. Next, he became increasingly apprehensive of going out of the house, of working, even of talking to other people. All these phobias made him very uptight. His life seemed to be closing up. He became blind to life. He just didn't want to continue it any more. Staying at home, he ruminated all day long on the unhappy relationships which he had gone through. And when he did work, he became furious because his partners didn't see things the way he did. One morning, on the way to work, he fell asleep driving. Traffic was bumper-to-bumper. And he kept dozing off, thinking that as long as he knew he was dozing off, he wouldn't fall asleep. The last thing he told himself was that, if he should fall asleep and have an accident, he would fall into good hands. Well, he did fall asleep, and leaning on the horn, abruptly he woke up to the shock of his own car hitting the median strip. Somehow he managed to steer the car back into the lane and then to edge off to the right shoulder of the road. If he had wanted to die, this would have been a perfect opportunity, he said to himself.

Another horn had blown as well, however; and he knew something had to be done. He decided to attend a workshop where people were allowed to bring out their grief and anger. There he discovered other people's problems. A man from Holland talked about the war, how he still continued to relive the horrors of that time, how the occupiers shot his brothers and mistreated his mother and sister. A mother whose daughter had shot herself eight months ago was also there. After listening to these stories he felt quite ashamed to say that he was simply afraid to leave the house. Sorrow can become a link with other people and open us up to them. Sorrow can melt down our self-centredness, and free us from judging and accusing others.

At the same workshop he discovered much anger in himself, especially against his father, who had left home after he was born. He tried to overcome this anger with his father, his stepfather, his mother, and the nun from the third grade. He wrote to his father that he didn't hate him for anything and that he loved him for nothing. The fear of flying, the fear of leaving the house, the drive to let go of his own life not only were stopped but were replaced with the forgiveness which 'offers all things'. Only inner reconciliation with our own parents, even after their death, can heal our phobias and fears and destructiveness. Only forgiveness opens the gates of the future and restores in us the love of life.

And now it is his pleasure to help others. Because he is a cook, he works with blind people to teach them to cook, showing them how to make a soufflé by touching and how to flambé by listening to the sizzle in the pan. In preparing to teach these cooking skills, he worked for three days in his own restaurant with a blindfold. He also works with the terminally ill, developing a new cuisine to stimulate their lessening appetites. From all this he has learned many things, because as he gave more of himself, he learned more about himself.

And now he has found his way, on the other side of immobilizing fears, far beyond accumulated anger and discouragement. Now his eyes light up when he starts to talk about salmon with a colourful garnish of shredded zucchini and thinly sliced apples, sauced with yogurt and herbs – the menu today for one of his patients. Nothing that happened to him has been useless; on the contrary, it has all become the rich material with which he builds up his inner home. His hurts and wounds have become treasures of healing for others. As a celebration of life, he offered me a salad of fresh melon and strawberries on a dark green lettuce leaf dressed with maple syrup, orange juice and fresh lemon.

Truly, God never abandons a child who crawls into the bushes to pray.

(4) A Son To His Parents

> 'Give, and it will be given to you. A good measure, pressed down, shaken together and running over, will be poured into your lap. For with the measure you use, it will be measured to you.'
>
> *Luke 6.38*

For their golden wedding anniversary my parents invited all their children and grandchildren to a dinner in town. During the dinner everybody present was expected to make a presentation. One read Psalm 121; another told some stories with a light touch; one of my sisters presented a collage of old photographs; the grandchildren presented a skit. Only rarely before had we been able to express our gratitude in words; a certain sense of discretion forbade this. How could we have expressed our admiration? One needs one's whole life to thank. Since then my parents have passed away, but each word I said at the dinner is more true now than ever.

'Your life and the love which is its seal, the love you give, the love you receive, are as a woven cloth whose colours on a day like today are being admired. This cloth, woven by you together with the gifts of each other and worn together, has slowly lost its wrinkles during the years in which you yourself became older.

'At the outset you didn't know what you would be weaving. The day you started, perhaps you still thought of a model, of a predestined pattern. What dream did you hide in yourself at that time? What did you dream? Maybe you thought: it will be deep blue or it will be like morning mist, like the early dew or like sharp sunlight and transparent skies on a late afternoon.

'Doesn't it take years before the true colours of life reveal themselves – and not as dreams seemed to predict but on a deeper level, wrought by suffering, the burdens of every day, the perseverance in courage, by some grey monotony and by the ever new beginnings, by the worries and the pain?

'One has to carry much before knowing that one is carried. One has to realize one's own colour and rejoice in seeing the other's colour. One has to cling again and again to the thread of the other – not only the splendid ones but also the invisible, the hidden ones – so as not to break off one's own filament.

'The threads in your lives had to be woven in the life of others, with patient hands, before the harmony of your own heart could appear. So many, close by and far away, mingle their colours in your pattern. They sometimes expect that their entangled or confused threads can find in you their unity and become a continuous fabric of stripes.

'And so your life is an echo of the old chant: I praise you for the wonder of myself, for the wonder of your works, you watched when I was being formed in secret, knitted together in the limbo of the womb.

'We discern so little of the harmony of the other, and we lack clear-sightedness, the fruit of simplicity and surrender. We colour the other with ourselves because we are not free from ourselves. But in spite of this, God harmonizes human chords; God pulls us together with lead-strings of love. Thus is your life and the love which is its seal, the love you give, the love you receive, as a woven cloth that adorns you with God.

'Sustained and carried forward by each other as you are, there is a stillness in you, the stillness of surrender, uncovered in the secret of your hidden life. There is the deepest accord. There too you offer praise. And wherever praise of God takes over, life rises, colours blossom, golden threads shine out, and an aura of peacefulness surrounds everyone near you.

'That offering of praise – no longer as the dew that quickly disappears, no longer as the morning mist that conceals the contours of sorrow and struggles – is the softened evening light whose warmth surrounds us and whose touch caresses us where wounds have contaminated our inner home. That offering of praise reconciles and illumines the woven lines of your life.'

(5) 'I Say Thank You a Lot For The World'

> At that time Jesus, full of joy through the Holy Spirit, said, 'I praise you, God of heaven and earth, because you have hidden these things from the wise and learned, and revealed them to little children.'
>
> *Luke 10.21*

During a retreat led by the New York brothers of Taizé, held at Koinonia, a Lutheran camp in the vicinity of New York City, a young man who had gone through a lot in his life stood up and said:

'There is a point when you get desperate enough. When you really get desperate enough, your faith takes over and tilts you because the whole thing of Christianity is based on faith. And always in blind faith. That's real hard for other people to understand, particularly if you have an intellectual bent and you lean towards that. I struggle with it a lot and I think to myself: I have to believe because I know that it is true. I have friends who want to argue, and I say: Don't argue with me about it. I can't argue it. How can I argue this? It is either something you do or you don't do. That's it.

'So when I pray, I say thank you. I say thank you a lot for the world. How beautiful it is. I just get overwhelmed with how beautiful it is, to look at trees, at the sky, to look at clouds and rain, to look at snow. I always say: Oh please God, don't let them tear it up and destroy it. It's wonderful, thank you for it. And I give thanks always for my health, and my joy, and for everything that I have, for my existence, for my being. And I give thanks to God for God, and I ask God to be blessed, because . . . you know. And I try not to ask.

'I never for a moment doubted that there was love some place.'

(6) The Only Dance There Is

> 'Everyone who drinks this water will be thirsty
> again, but whoever drinks the water I give will
> never thirst. Indeed, the water I give will
> become a spring of water welling up to eternal
> Life.'
>
> *John 4.13–14*

While listening to a person it happens that an image
emerges inside of oneself, an image of the hidden other.
We all carry façades behind which we hide our wounded
intimacy. At the same time we long to be recognized and
known for who we are. So it is a gift when suddenly the
beauty of the other can be revealed and communicated.

In the person I met one morning in a renovated house
filled with antiques in Maine I saw almost immediately
a life waiting for pure and unconditional love; a life
waiting to set out for a dance, a dance of exultation. We
had met in several places but only this morning, sitting
in his kitchen on long-legged bar stools, did we open up.
Relationships have always been important to him. The
reason he gives is that at home there had never been any
heart-felt relationships whatsoever. His stepfather and
mother never expressed their feelings in front of him,
maybe never had feelings at all. No one ever, ever said to
him: I love you. He was an illegitimate child, and in the
thirties, during the depression, his Polish Catholic
mother had nowhere to go but to a home for unwed
mothers run by the Salvation Army (each time he speaks
about his mother he says: 'Bless her heart').

He saw his father maybe four or five times in his life,
and he expected to feel some sense of connection, but
each meeting was a disaster. Was he angry? On the

surface, certainly not. Kids accept; they can never say no, even if they are fourteen or fifteen years old. He just went looking for his own self. He took off and started to travel around the country. Miami, New York, Montreal. Like other fifteen-year-old kids, he made his living off the street, selling the only thing he had to sell. For him it was not so bad. Even today he thinks it was OK. 'You can be just fine. I'm OK, I'm OK, as much as anybody can be OK.' But while affirming this he still looks like he is carrying a terrible weight, a burden which he is unable to throw off his soul.

It is on a deeper level that he is 'OK'. Every time I had met him I had been impressed by his deep yearning, his longing for pure love. He immediately reacts by saying that this longing is in everyone, and it surely is. But it remains, nevertheless, my vision of him.

'One is never OK.' I say, 'unless one lives dancingly, like King David before the Ark of God.' He answers that, for the wounded, healing is the only dance there is. Therefore he has been involved in a hospice. He sees the need to connect people with the last part of their life, in spite of their fear that there is nothing on the other side. He is convinced that people can discover a wholeness at that point of their existence and can become who they really are. Of course, he can't push this on people, and you are not supposed to do this in your hospice work. 'You can't rush up to the deathbed and offer them your Christ and beat them into conversion.' But what he asks them to do is to think of all the people they want to forgive, or who should be forgiven, and the people by whom they want to be forgiven.

For himself it is easy to love in an unconditional way somebody who is dying, because that person is not a threat. And he senses a wonderful wholeness about this.

He finds this wholeness in washing people, shaving them, cutting their toenails, cleaning them up or in just being there quietly, sometimes saying nothing. For him, to be there is in a sense prayer. 'You're living it.' To be there is 'to feel the Holy Spirit.'

Originally he offered to be a volunteer only, to drive people to medical appointments. He didn't want to become involved in such a way that he would be too enthusiastic about it. Two weeks later, he would have said: Why did I commit myself to this? He also had to take a course in listening. Halfway through, the director asked him to drive a woman to a doctor's appointment. She was dying of leukaemia. His original intention had been to work specifically with people who were homosexually orientated, but here he met a married woman whose husband had died of cancer also. During a whole year every Friday turned into a ritual. He would first take her to the doctor, then to the hairdresser, and finally he would buy some ice cream for her. And then they would drive to the ocean, just to sit there and to look, without any deep religious or philosophical discussions. 'Isn't this a lovely day? Isn't the water pretty? I used to swim when I was a girl.'

There was a real quiet understanding between them on the last day of her life. He went to see her at the hospital three times a day that week. That last morning he asked her if there was anything she would like. Some ice cream, she said. So he went out and brought her some ice cream and was feeding it to her. With each bite she looked at him, so lovingly, so purely and with such a wonderful smile. Then she said that she was tired. He took the ice cream away and she fell asleep, went into a coma and died.

He was sitting there quietly as she was dying, and, as

he does each time at that solemn moment of death, he gave thanks for all and everything this woman had brought into the world: joy, truth, honesty, beauty, everything she had given him up to that healing moment when she looked at him, so lovingly, so purely and with such a wonderful smile.

For all of us who are wounded, love is the only dance there is.

(7) Love's Likeness

> 'Before long, the world will not see me any-more, but you will see me. Because I live, you also will live.'
>
> *John 14.19*

For one year I was the spiritual companion of two young adults. The young woman was dying of cancer. While loving and being loved converged in them, she prepared her friend for her own death by letting go of him and by enabling him to let go of her. In the face of death their affinity had to be transformed in its orientation. Their human love, they said, had to become God's: to return to its origin and to be anchored in another dimension, invisible but eternal. Their question was: how can we let our love flow into the love of God? After her death I wanted to describe to her parents in a letter how I saw their evolution:

The audacity of their encounter found its origin in the fact that together they wanted to live an image, an 'icon' of her imminent, radiant encounter with Christ. This icon of love was the key to the limitless polyphony through which they expressed their togetherness. Of course, in opening up a way for the other to go forward, a way of growth and of faithfulness, they walked on unique, unknown and sometimes shaky ground; there was no way for them to avoid the imprint of their personalities.

But this melody continued to surround them, hour after hour, through the whole year, strengthened as they were by an inner certainty and conviction which did not come from themselves. Taking root in this melody, they were led into a mutual birthing so as to accompany each other on the road of their different destinations.

Living an inner festival while facing the imminence of death created in them not only an attitude of strong solidarity concerning the down-to-earth reality of their lives, but also an attitude of renunciation. Those two poles did not exclude one another; on the contrary, each lay at the heart of the other, each begetting the other.

In appearance they seemed to be limited – but fundamentally were enriched – by their friends near or far who became involved in the widening radius of their adventure. They were also limited – but, on another level, deeply blessed – by the impossibility of expressing fully, in an autonomous way, the sharing of their lives.

The gift of oneself is always partial with regard to Christ's endless self-giving: it can't be more than a frail image. Because of the dynamics of the unknown, there was a danger of lapsing from mutual welcome and the gratuitous gift of love into reciprocal appropriation, from interior intensity into an explicit abundance of express-ions, giving their encounter a different aspect. But they received just what they needed – in itself inexhaustible – to live together in fullness.

If their encounter allowed them, for the time being, to sustain one another in the depth and the breadth of their lives, with joy and much cheerfulness, today, in the dimension of eternity, the longing of each for the other has been fulfilled.

(8) A Lamp Is Lit

> 'Like the lamp, let your light shine before everyone.'
>
> *Matthew 5.16*

It happened in Southern California. I had just given an introduction to the work in small groups that was part of a retreat. The retreat was one of the stops of the 'pilgrimage of reconciliation' led by two other brothers of Taizé and myself. The question the small groups were invited to work on was: 'What fascinates me in Jesus – whom we believe rises in every person who suffers? Out of which void, suffering, or need have I become vulnerable to that life-giving aspect of Christ's life?' During the break a woman, with a baby on her arm, took me aside to tell me 'one of those born-again things,' as she put it. In a few minutes time – we were interrupted by somebody else's announcement through the microphone – I was transplanted from my happy introduction to that zone of desperation which slumbers under thick blankets of everyone's conscience. Only here desperation had already been turned into courage, and even surrender.

In listening one has to go under with the other, underneath the differences in experience and choices, struggling with the same many-headed monsters and recognizing them as one's own, before being able, maybe long afterwards, to rise to the surface. In listening, the 'I' of the narrator has to be espoused by the 'you' of the listener; the story's quotation marks become superfluous because the listener has uncovered in himself or herself the same shaky ground. However, even on Good Friday the church, completely darkened, keeps one candle lit. There is always a light.

She had been raised an Episcopalian but had been through an agnostic period in college. Later, she married a Jewish friend who had many relatives. So if there was a death in the family, they went to church or synagogue, but never out of need. But something happened to her, after living through four very tense years in her marriage, 'a period of hell,' as she called it.

Her husband had been very unhappy with himself and very suicidal, and she had been herself contaminated by this suicidal drive. He often had breakdowns, waking her in the middle of the night, screaming and yelling; he also needed many relationships with other women. She concentrated all her efforts on trying to heal them both, on getting back together and on forgiving. 'I had my lesson for forgiving in my marriage.' She thought they had worked out their problems before they decided to start again, moving to the East Coast where they had bought a store which had such promise. Also, she had become pregnant and was thrilled about it. She hadn't been pregnant for the four years of their marriage because he didn't want a child. But then he said 'yes' for a moment. Although he later changed his mind, she didn't. She wanted her child.

In the middle of the move, they were staying with her parents in her home town. During that month her husband went off and had a fling with one of her closest childhood friends. At that moment she reached rock bottom, what she calls 'total hell, where it was dark and everything was gone.' Her dear friend and her husband –

whom she thought was coming back – all the promise, all the hope, all the future was gone. She remembers going downtown to the church in which she had been raised. Because that church was locked, she tried the Catholic church which was open. She went in there and started praying. Although she had no faith any more, no religion, no experience, nothing, this force came out, 'inside out.' She hadn't known she could even choose to pray. And this force was saying in her: 'Christ, I give myself over to you. Christ, I give myself over to you.' She remembers becoming embarrassed because of all those feelings coming up all of a sudden, because of the total peace that hit her and a mystical feeling of awe and surrender. She says that if you go through something like that with Christ, you can never go back to that emptiness again. Once your heart has opened, it is open for good, no matter how foolish you may be, or stupid, or blind. 'It can't close up from here; it just carries me forward.'

Yes, if you turn your life over and enter into a living relationship with Christ, you have a whole respect for life, you feel respected, you have this sublime love without threat, without hurt. Problems remain, but you belong; immense struggles lie ahead but praying heals, praying brings about reconciliation. For the wounded, especially, prayer is that one candle in the darkness, always alight.

(9) The Womb of All Beginning

> '. . . the tender mercy of our God, by which the rising sun will come to us from heaven to shine on those living in darkness and in the shadow of death . . .'
>
> *Luke 1.78–79*

I have spent every New Year's Eve for almost ten years now in a European cathedral. One New Year's Eve I was in Cologne where the European youth meeting, led by the Community of Taizé, was held.

Standing on the Rhine bridge, I saw the cathedral's silvery silhouette glistening like a mirage of some elfin castle, its pinnacles plunging into the deep to catch the trail of falling fireworks. But the fairy-like phantom, all shining and moving in the river, quickly dissolved its magic as I approached and looked up towards the massive height of the cathedral.

Was the cathedral of Cologne built to carry away, to lift up, to transport into ecstasy as an enraptured predecessor of the future, less mystical skyscraper? Or to oppress, to weigh down and to frighten as an armoured fortification, entrenched more deeply in earthly pursuits than in heaven's roots? Many elements inside the cathedral conveyed the impression of a funereal monument, a tomb: the darkened windows, the blind eyes of prophets and saints standing on the brink of perilous socles, the haze in the choir-lofts, the people's breath floating away into the high vaults, the pervading winter cold keeping the pillars and capitals from tumbling down, and above all the immobile shrine of the Magi guarded by a half-moon of crescent chapels.

Why did I feel so cold inside? As a modern Tantalus reaching out for water to drink and for fruit to eat, I discovered only that the spring tide of my days had receded and that fruition would require more and more renunciations. In the silence, staring at this void clothed by vaults, sad memories welled up. On all the New Year's Eves of my childhood the minister read aloud the names of those who had died, indicating their ages. Like a last honour guard we stood up, remembering. Today the list would contain many much loved names.

So as a child I knew about this fact of facts: that one day the lives of human beings come to an end; that every day one is alone; that one day a beloved person whom one had seen so lively and adorned with a light in her eyes so pure and strong, lies down in an untouchable and unspeakable aloofness. One day, riding on a bicycle across town; one day, lying down because of sudden pain; one day, disconnected in a hospital room – those people who were once full of you and looked upon you with speechless joy, in a sudden change now yield their spirit. Every day one is abandoned on this side of the horizon.

But then, as I finally kneel in the cathedral of Cologne, in a stream of images there appears a garden – a garden in Oregon, high above the Columbia River Valley. In the twilight I find delight in the soft breeze. Around ferns and towering fir trees 'busy Lizzies' have woven tapestries of red flowers. Walking among the garden's fifty-eight California redwoods I almost stumble on a small marble tombstone, illumined only by the glowing sunset. The balancing redwoods and seguoias face each other like perfectly aligned pillars, rhododendrons in all colours embellish what seem to be the nave and the choir, and the sunset takes the place of the apse.

At the far end of this natural cathedral, on a high pedestal, I face a statue made of white Carrara marble, vandalized, its arms broken. Marble shines up, and I read on the plinth at the foot of the risen Christ this poem: 'Christ has no hands but our hands to do his work today. He has no feet but our feet to lead you in his way. He has no tongue but our tongue to tell people how he died. He has no help but our help to bring people to his side.'

It then dawns upon me, on New Year's Day, that beyond each tombstone and beyond each broken life, a new horizon opens up, incessantly, on which stands the paschal victim, both tomb in whom we die and womb of all beginning.

(10) Singing As Spirituality

> Immediately the blind man received his sight and followed Jesus, praising God. When all the people saw it, they also praised God.
>
> *Luke 18.43*

Singing is one of the best expressions of praise. At a convention of pastoral musicians in Ohio, all five thousand participants gathered together for the final Eucharist. Acolytes advanced towards the altar from four directions. They held in their hands long, slender bamboo sticks to which coloured strips of cloth were attached. The sticks bent and bowed and the strips danced in the air. The priests, the choir and the soloists stood on the platform, waiting. A cantor intoned the chant. During the long entrance rite we sang again and again one single verse adapted from the second letter to Timothy: 'We rely on the power of God.' The acolytes arrived at the centre of the room; we then felt as if everybody was present from East and West and North and South. The choir struck up the refrain, the congregation repeated it, men and women alternately sang it again and again. The greeting of the presider started out with the same refrain sung by him alone. The opening prayer took the same theme up again. For twenty minutes we were penetrated down to our depths by this meditative chant before entering into the liturgy of the Word and of the Eucharist.

In many church traditions, singing touches people more than anything else. Listen to Methodists singing together 'Oh, for a Thousand Tongues to Sing,' look at their faces, look at the way they stand up with the hymnal in their hands, look at their concentration. They are so present during the singing because they learned the hymn in their childhood: their past joins this moment of praise. Sometimes I happen to look at the brothers in the community I belong to when we sing in the church at Taizé, especially in the evening when the lights have been dimmed, and it seems to me as if children stood there, as if they suddenly had recovered their childhood. A deep reconciliation takes place in singing. Listen to Lutherans in a packed cathedral singing 'A Mighty Fortress Is Our God.' Look at black liturgies. Look at Catholics singing 'Be Not Afraid.' Singing is the zenith of our spiritual life. Singing as spirituality is accessible to all. Who doesn't like to sing, or at least to listen to singing? In secularized countries in Europe the 'song-and-praise' shows on TV are for millions the only contact left with church life. Millions of people fulfil their Sunday obligation by pushing the button of their television, and humming along during the show. Are there houses in the world were Christmas carols are forbidden to enter?

Singing, with thousands, in a small group or alone, is praying. Prayers have to be sung. If prayers are spoken, in our own words or even in the words of the tradition, they somehow have first to be understood; intellectually, they have to convince us. While singing we can involve all our energies in the offering of the prayer, in the act of praying. Another problem with spoken prayers, with improvised prayers particularly is that we are very much present ourselves with our twists and peculiarities. Some people pray too fluently and others need to have recourse to standard formulas in order to fill up the gaps in their own thoughts. Only black and charismatic liturgies use spoken prayers as a take-off. Their prayers may start on a rational level, the words may at first be quietly aligned. But after some time the thread is lost; the prayers rise up in sounds and stirrings before breaking through the sound barrier by singing.

Singing brings us to the highest levels of praise. Singing places us on the true axis of faith. As the Shakers, so strong in inspirational gift-songs, sang, 'T'is the Gift to come down where we ought to be, / And when we find ourselves in the place just right, / 'T'will be in the valley of Love and Delight!' Discussion about faith, theology, commitments of all kinds are important for the growth of our faith, but they are secondary in comparison with the act of praise, the act of faith in singing.

Singing penetrates into the lowest levels of the unconscious. Singing expels demons. It frees us from all our enemies. It makes us enter into a space of simplicity and freedom. 'I have come to sweep the house of the Lord / Clean, clean, for I've come / And I've not come in vain. / With my broom in my hand, / With my fan and my flail.' Self-analysis, psychology, therapies of all kinds are important for the understanding of our faith, but they are secondary in comparison with the act of exorcism, the act of hope in singing.

Singing opens up to the gift of community in all its breadth. Singing is the miracle of voices blending together. It reveals the inside of our being together, the motivation of our common struggles. Singing has a centripetal force. 'Build Me a House, saith the Lord, / And let every heart contribute / As you raise it to My Spirit. / With My Glory I will fill it / And My Power shall be round about.' Group processes, sociology, experiences of all kinds are important for the consequences of our faith; but they are only secondary in comparison with the miracle of community, the act of love in singing.

Personally, I am not particularly musical but I sing every day. I sing the first word I pronounce in the morning. I sing in church, in community, in faith, hope and love. Song and praise have taught me happiness.

(11) 'My Walk With God Is Glorious'

> 'You are going to have the light just a little while longer. Walk while you have the light before darkness overtakes you. The person who walks in the dark does not know where he or she is going. Put your trust in the light while you have it, so that you may become children of light.'
>
> *John 12.35–36*

A friend and I travelled back to San Francisco after a long visit to a home for teenagers in the area. He is a middle-aged man, elegantly dressed, who could have been dandy-like had he not refrained. Vaguely Methodist because of his upbringing, he has given a secular twist to his life. I didn't know much about him. But suddenly, just before the exit for Millbrae, he said: 'Here is a thing that amazes me, a thing that keeps me from falling completely under the sway of cynicism. My walk with God is glorious.' 'What did you say?' I ask. I am astonished. How many middle-aged men would tell you this, in the middle of traffic, returning home after a day of work? How many people in their fifties still have the courage to remain faithful, in spite of frustrations, depressions and disorderliness, to the innocence of loving God? And myself? Don't I live sometimes as if I wanted to slam the door on the very gifts I have received?

Over the last miles we had talked about the young people we had met. They were like modern lepers. One of the teenagers had seen his mother commit suicide. He was brought into the home for kids, and he settled in very quickly. He loved it there. In three months a foster home had been lined up for him. A week or so before he was supposed to go he had a complete schizophrenic breakdown and in the process of the next eight months that he stayed in the home he was very, very sick. Another teenager there gets very good grades at school and will probably go to university. But she is suicidal. Her arms bear scars of razor cuts. She has been in the hospital many times. She has a chronic heart problem and can't be left alone. At night she has to sleep in the women's house and be hugged all night.

'What is our leprosy?' we ask ourselves. Aren't we as much lepers as these young people? The leprosies of our time are inside; they are apathy, indifference and hypocrisy. Knowing that one cannot help the person who has fallen out of society produces cynicism, burnout, apathy. When one tries to change things, to transform unjust structures in society or to deal with the people who are the products of a collapsing society, one discovers that one cannot do much. One turns away from the suffering on people's faces. One looks into the window of a store, one buries one's head behind *The Wall Street Journal*, one moves into a different neighbourhood. One dilutes oneself into thinking everything is rosy.

Because my friend has felt cynical and has suffered

from the hypocrisy around him, he is as astonished as I am that he is now able to celebrate the presence of God in his own heart. But this inner celebration is genuine; it allows him to see the face of Jesus in people who suffer. His family accuses him of romantic idealism, of a Pollyanna view of reality. But he recognizes that he is called to work hard for reconciliation, wherever he can, God cannot just give it. But wherever people reconcile themselves God is there. Wherever we set out over and over again, refusing apathy, cynicism and hypocrisy, God walks with us. Hard work – without knowing the outcome; trust – leaving the outcome in God's hands.

(12) The Fecundity of Faith

> A man scatters seed on the land; he goes to bed at night and gets up in the morning, and the seed sprouts and grows – how, he does not know.
>
> *Mark 4.26–27*

The most important gifts in life come like fruit falling from a tree. They are there, suddenly, ripe in the mellow air, unexpected. We torment ourselves, seeing no results from all our efforts and longings. But then comes this surprise carrying us away beyond our doubts, and we marvel.

A friend in New York who works in a hospital told his spiritual director about his visits with the patients – how important those visits had been to him and how transforming for him as well as for many of the patients. The spiritual director answered: What has happened to you is that you have been transformed by God so that when you look at those people, it is God who looks at them, and that is what they see. There is a line in Ecclesiasticus (17.8) which says that God puts God's own 'eye' in your heart so that you will see the glory of God and show others the magnificence of God's works.

My friend would have preferred the gift of wisdom, the gift to distinguish illusion from reality. Wisdom, I'm sure, would not have been bad either, but instead he received 'God's own light.'

In the Mass – he is a priest – he used to say: 'May we receive him with hearts filled with joy. May this joy become a light with which we see people with new eyes.' Now he says: 'May this joy become a light so that everyone whom we meet will see themselves as God sees them.'

'How did it come about?' I asked him. 'I didn't do it', he replied, 'it just happened; I mean, I didn't know that that was true.'

Your faith bears fruit. The years pass, and you don't see it. One day, when you least expect it, the seed sprouts and grows.

(13) Prayers After Compline

> 'No one who has left home or brothers or sisters or mother or father or children or fields for me and the gospel will fail to receive a hundred times as much in this present age (homes, brothers, sisters, mothers, children and fields – and with them, persecutions) and in the age to come, eternal life.'
>
> *Mark 10.29–30*

Monks in Oregon invited me to join in their prayers after Compline. What is a monk? Monks are people who burn all bridges behind them in order to be as totally dependent on Christ as possible. Following Christ to God, they consent to be drastically simplified and peacefully brought to unity by praying. Others will consent to be stretched, divided into a thousand pieces, becoming everything to everyone through so doing. Monks are thirsty for only one thing, monks want to witness to the priority of God above everything else. So they pray ceaselessly and endlessly, they have organized their life in such a way that nothing is left but prayer alone. Even if in their humanness they attach themselves to the animals they have to care for, to their jars of marmalade or to illuminated manuscripts, even if they settle down in the routine of tight prayer and work schedules, their life in its entirety has been consecrated to Christ. Even if they go through the most severe crises and suffer attacks from legions of demons, their life is full of the unseen God. It is enriching to stay with people who don't want to possess.

The old monks and I shuffle along the walls of long corridors, and a bell rings. The world may hang on to its talk-shows, the world may cling to its pleasures, the world may vanish overnight like a universal Titanic. Here it is time for ecstasy. The monks bow down on kneelers. A signal is given. In a self-sufficient world, bowing monks venerate the mysteries of life, the sources of creation, the marvels of God. Tonight, after compline, with a bouquet of trilliums, white and green, up front and a smell of the myrtlewood tree all around, we say a long litany to Mary. The Latin acclamations are so brief that all my attention is absorbed by the attempt to keep the rhythm without giving the awkward impression of not knowing how to handle this liturgical extravaganza. Each acclamation is followed by the forceful drum of our simultaneous '*ora pro nobis*' (pray for us). As soon as I enter into the rhythm, the prayer becomes an incantatory mantra espousing the pulsations of my heart. The continual repetition of the refrain and the succession of brief invocations convey the impression of some futuristic music in which the freedom of an ecstatic soloist is moderated by the regulated pattern of a volley of tomtoms. I'm struck by the primitiveness of this prayer form and by the poverty of the monks. But somehow my heart is not in it.

Later in the evening I walk in the garden, still haunted by the ritual recitation. The lilies – symbol of Mary – grow wild all through the woods around the cloister. Saint Joseph stands here with his staff abloom with lilies because, as the tradition goes, he is supposed to have been chosen as Mary's spouse from among many young men.

I have never been led to pray to Mary but even the theologians of my youth taught that she was the epitome of the communion of saints. They skirmished with Mariologists but nevertheless recognized Mary as the mother of Christ. I was inhibited about praying to Mary until I entered the Community of Taizé and appreciated the significance of the icon of the Virgin which adorns the church. But only after my own mother died did I come close to the mystery of Mary. Therefore, on this evening, far from home, far from the lamplight above a friend's table, I pray as a way of entering into communion with my mother, sisters and friends, and with all I love:

> Mother of Jesus,
> Mother most favoured,
> Mother after our heart,

Mother from generation to generation,
Mother of our mothers,
Mother of every longing,
Mother of all tears,
Mother of justice,
Mother of the poor,
Mother of humanity,
Mother of the Redeemer,
Mother of the Church,
Virgin most lovely,
Virgin most open-hearted,
Virgin most sisterly,
Virgin most tender,
Virgin most serene,
Virgin most free,
Mirror of women,
Treasure of compassion,
Root of tenderness,
Gift of presence,
Voice of praise,
Bloom of hope,
Source of strength,
Heart of gold,
Ark of the homeless,
Port of heaven,
Star of the lonely,
Refuge in distress,
Consolation of the bereaved,
Help of the innocent,
Servant of the Holy Spirit,
Servant of angels,
Servant of your people,
Servant of the oppressed,
Servant of martyrs,

Servant of the handicapped,
Servant of the dying,
Servant of lost souls,
Servant of reconciliation,
Servant of peace,
Servant of your servants,
Servant of the Lord Jesus,
Servant of God, pray for us.

This evening it is by praying as a son to Mary that I learn again to know that I have not been abandoned, that I too am welcomed and loved at this very moment.

(14) Christ Welcomes You With Such Joy

> 'I am going there to prepare a place for you.'
> *John 14.2*

In an inner room of a house we cannot see, we are met by the welcoming Christ. All we need, all we desire is here, already in our hearts, 'not what is infinitely remote but what is nearest at hand.'

Where we stand, where we hide, where we fall and fall again, where we are perplexed or jubilant, Christ is there. Only there can we live fully, discover behind the façade of fears the firmness of love, and carry the burdens and the blessings of people close to us and those not yet close to us.

Under the roof of this dwelling, Christ fashions the true shape of our being. In its inner room we can never feel abandoned: Christ's love welcomes us.

2

The Downward Ascent

Jesus, I live to Thee,
The loveliest and best;
My life in Thee, Thy life in me,
In Thy blest love I rest.

Jesus I die to Thee,
Whenever death shall come;
To die in Thee is life to me
In my eternal home.

Whether to live or die,
I know not which is best;
To live in Thee is bliss to me,
To die is endless rest.

Living or dying, Lord,
I ask but to be Thine;
My life in Thee, Thy life in me,
Makes heaven forever mine.

– Old hymn of the German Reformed Church in
Pennsylvania, written by Henry Harbough in
1850.

(1) The Ark in a Drowned World

> As soon as Jesus was baptized, he went up out of the water. At that moment heaven was opened.
>
> *Matthew 3.16*

I arrived at Port Authority, the huge bus station on 42nd Street in New York, in the middle of the night. It was freezing cold outside, so cold that the city had ordered the bus station to let the street people come in. Hundreds and hundreds of homeless people, de-institutionalized mental patients, shopping-bag ladies and other specimens of New York's night fauna had crowded the entrance hall, occupied the sparse seats on the lower levels and transformed the waiting areas into an infernal abode for departed souls. It was three o'clock in the morning, and people slept on the floor covered with newspapers and cardboard boxes, lying around half-naked, satisfying their needs in public or staring motionlessly into the nothingness of some fugitive vision. Many talked aloud to themselves, walking back and forth at a frenzied pace. It was the scene of a drowned world.

I had just come from a nice visit to a well-dressed bishop in Connecticut. I had my bag with me with money in it and airline tickets, I feared the threatening looks of some mentally disturbed who rushed up to me talking incoherently and grimacing crazily. I couldn't help but think, however, of Jesus' question to his disciples: 'You had not the strength to stay with me for one hour?' What else do I exist for, what else is there to do than to immerse myself in this wilderness, waiting for whatever these people are waiting for? They are waiting for an ark, I'm sure, which they could board in order to prevent the flood of disasters from submerging them even further. They are waiting for a covenant between them and us. I walked around, wrestling with myself, before coming to the conclusion that I couldn't. I couldn't. I simply didn't have the inner strength to stay there in that apocalyptic atmosphere. I didn't have the fire, I didn't have the Spirit to drown myself in this Jordan of 42nd Street. And I went home.

Jesus is the ark. Jesus immersed himself in the darkness of sin around him, in the evil of the world, in the hopelessness of an apocalyptic time. Did he know that he would survive? Jesus had no Jesus to project on to. He was the first to set the pattern. His pattern was the down-and-up of his baptism, the immersion in the Jordan, the piercing by the Holy Spirit, the confirmation by God. The incarnation doesn't work from on high but enters from below. Jesus went downward, immersed himself in the oppositions with powers and principalities in both an outer and an inner way, immersed himself in suffering and death and by doing so established a new Covenant. His baptism announced his cross. Both events expressed Jesus' drowning, both signified his own descent into an infernal world. And what emerged was the kingdom, was the ark and the covenant, was the rainbow in the clouds, was the opened heaven and the resurrection. Since then there is no end of the age any more, no apocalypse, no drowned world because the kingdom's ripples are moving, salvation is at hand, everything descended will ascend, God is at work stopping the springs of the deep and the sluices of heaven. God is going to set a bow in the clouds for the homeless and the mentally disturbed and for every species in the fauna of New York. God is going to open the hatch of the ark and look out; God is going to open heaven for all those people who haven't seen anything else around but hell.

But each time I pass through the entrance hall of Port Authority, God grapples with me, God struggles with my freedom – because this is not creation, this is not the kingdom, this is close to hell. Don't go home.

(2) A Daunting Faith, a Haunting Face

> Then Peter remembered the word Jesus had spoken to him: 'Before the rooster crows twice, you will disown me three times.' And he broke down and wept.
>
> *Mark 14.72*

Shusako Endo, the Japanese novelist, describes in one of his books the persecution of Portuguese missionaries in seventeenth-century Japan. One of them, Sebastian Rodrigues, came to Japan with an immense missionary task: to sustain persecuted Japanese Christians and to capture the country and its culture for Christ. And to motivate him in his extreme adventure, the face of Christ had been present to him ever since he started to plan this mission. 'This face is deeply ingrained in my soul,' he says, 'the most beautiful, the most precious thing in the world has been living in my heart.'

But now he meets his former Portuguese seminary professor and evangelistic predecessor on Japanese soil. Forced into persecution of his own former co-religionists, the professor convinces his former student, after many tortures and torments, to trample on a large wooden plaque, called a *fumie*. Such a *fumie* was one of the psychological means used by the persecutors to bring Christians to denial. A copper medal was fixed to the plaque. And on the medal the face of Christ shone forth. The persecutors knew that it was enough to convince Christians to place their foot on this face, enough to destroy their faith.

It is a haunting story of denial, of a daunting faith. But there is also an even more haunting description in a few words of what is at the heart of Christ's life and death. The Christ in bronze on the *fumie* suddenly speaks to the Portuguese priest, saying: 'It was to be trampled on that I was born into this world. It was to share human pain that I carried my cross.'

One shudders at the thought of how easily we fall, or could fall, into apostasy. I shudder at the thought that I too could be forced to deny what is the most intimate gift I carry in myself: the face of Christ. One shudders at the thought that it was not enough for Christ to be born in this world, to carry his cross and to become the victim of persecutions coming from outside. But he also offers himself to be trampled on by his disciples, because his love leads him to share their pain and their persecution. I shudder at the thought that forgiveness leads to this extreme.

Although we disown Christ in moments and years of indifference, although we abandon Christ in hours and cycles of rejection, although we trample on the purest gift we have ever received, although 'we are faithless, he keeps faith, for he cannot deny himself.' (2 Timothy 2. 13). Christ remains present, suffers with us and offers himself to be trampled on when at the shrill cock's crow we burst into tears. Christ's cross is there today in this abandonment as much as it was twenty centuries ago or in seventeenth-century Japan. We, too, kiss Christ with

the kiss of betrayal but that doesn't set him against us
who wrong him. He kisses us with a kiss of forgiveness so
that our betrayal, like Judas', 'be quite undone and never
more be done.'

(3) A Litany of the Cross

> When the centurion, who stood there in front of
> Jesus, heard his cry and saw how he died, he
> said, 'Surely, this man was the Son of God!'
>
> *Mark 15.39*

O crucified Jesus,
disgraced and forsaken,
because you beseech us to
    forgive those who wrong us;
on the cross you cry out
for us who grieve you
with misdeeds and disdain.

O crucified Jesus,
despised and unwanted,
because you invite us to be like
    children in your kingdom;
on the cross you welcome home
all of us who disavow you
in darkness and mistrust.

O crucified Jesus,
mocked and destitute,
because you yearn to share with
    us our creator in heaven;

on the cross you bind together
all of us who are separated from you
in haughtiness and dissension.

O crucified Jesus,
accused and forlorn,
because you open for us the way to
    trust and to give;
on the cross you yield yourself
to us who abandon you,
heartless and afraid.

O crucified Jesus,
exposed and exhausted,
because you nourish us with loaves
    and fishes;
on the cross you thirst
for us who shun you,
satiated with ourselves.

O crucified Jesus,
taunted and indicated,
because you hallow God's holy name;
on the cross you gave up your spirit
for us who disregard you,
with indifference and irony.

O crucified Jesus,
condemned and slaughtered,
because you free us from evil and death;
on the cross you entrust us
forever
                    to the heart of God.

(4) I Know That My Redeemer Lives

> 'What about you?' he asked. 'Who do you say I am?'
>
> *Mark 8.29*

Who are you? You are my Redeemer who precedes all people in the land of the living. You are the Suffering Servant who, rejected, did not reject those who rejected you and who calls us not to let people suffer the suffering we may have experienced. You alone lead us into the communion of God, the alpha and omega of eternity. You live in the heart of every human being, you work in the depths of the universe, you transfigure all our past. You welcome us into life, you accompany us in our loving, you struggle with us through the sighs and revolutions of our hearts, you suffer from our resistances and injustices, you forgive us now and at the hour of our death when we have nothing, nothing left.

You are the Redeemer of people who cry out, of those hundreds of homeless streaming into Port Authority freezing in the cold, of nations that have their occupiers' boots on their necks. You are the Redeemer of that farmer who shot himself, of those young blacks in Soweto, of children born crippled with heads as big as their whole body, of women and men tortured in a hundred countries in the world. You are not a prophet or God in some otherworldly nirvana. You are flesh and blood in those who suffer. You must be in agony with this terrible world. You must be continuously pierced to the heart. Why do you still have to be rejected, to be put to death all the time?

My desire for you awakens me at night and my heart beats at the rhythm of your knock at the door. When I

rise, I think of you as the child in Simeon's arms, still safe
but destined to suffer; I see you on that donkey, in
Mary's arms escaping Herod's horse hoofs, still cared for
but already considered a danger by the powerful. I
become silent when I listen to the purity of your words,
your way of penetrating the human heart, of arguing
with enemies and adversaries. I look at you writing in the
sand with that woman waiting over there. I do see
Lazarus coming out of his tomb. And although I am here
two thousand years later, whenever I rise, that knowledge in which I am rooted wells up in me: you are the
Redeemer of all.

One day, I may not know who you are any more; one
day, when I am ill with a sleeping mind or a failing body;
one day when I am facing my own death. And although I
may never be able to say who you are, you yourself
branded in my heart these words: I know that my
Redeemer lives.

(5) Mary's First Sorrow: The Prophecy of Simeon

> 'This child is destined to cause the falling and
> rising of many in Israel, and to be a sign that
> will be spoken against, so that the thoughts of
> many hearts will be revealed. And a sword will
> pierce your own soul too.'
>
> *Luke 2.34–35*

I grieve for you, Mother, for the pain in your heart at the
prophecy of Simeon.

In the middle of the winter you had given birth to your
baby, so jolly with his little hands, so tranquil and quiet

in your arms. Your neighbours said that he looked like you. The same pure eyes! Was wartime the reason why you wanted first of all to present your baby at the temple? Was it because of the angel's greeting almost a year ago? Or simply because you wanted to tell of the greatness of God? Still weak, you stood up, looked for woollen blankets, wrapped them around your baby and rushed to the temple. Above all you wanted to make sure that your child would live, saved and safe. You and your people had had more than your share of scorn, more than your share of jeers. And this was your first baby, a son for whom you leapt for joy. 'Oh God,' you prayed, 'you dealt so wonderfully with me.'

When you entered the temple with all those blankets, your baby cried and you soothed him while lifting your eyes to God, in gratitude and love. Looking up to the Creator and looking after the Son, you were filled with the Spirit. But joy and sorrow go together, and you felt the long, long way you had to go. For a brief moment you felt overwhelmed by all the dangers that could arise before your child and against him, danger in the towns, dangers from the occupiers and from your own people, dangers from tortures, dangers from brigands and soldiers, dangers from all those crosses along the roads, dangers from condemnations and premature death.

Simeon, however, praised you and blessed you. He took your baby in his arms to hold him before God. You agreed wholeheartedly, you knew that this child was destined for God. He had found a home in your womb – and it certainly had been a surprise – but now your son was God's son. That's what Simeon said in his sermon: that in this little child God took sides with your people, that deliverance was now close, that persecution would end in full view of all the nations. You were full of wonder at what was being said about your child. But after the worship service you talked with your husband about what Simeon had meant when he spoke about rejection and fall. You didn't understand but you felt a strange pain in your heart, recalling how King David had shuddered and burst into tears when he heard the news of his son's death and how all your people had lamented again and again when the vine was pining away and the merry lyre was silent.

I grieve for you, Mother, for the sudden pain in your heart at the prophecy of Simeon.

(6) Second Sorrow: The Flight Into Egypt

> 'Get up, take the child and his mother and escape to Egypt. Stay there until I tell you, for Herod is going to search for the child to kill him.'
>
> *Matthew 2.13*

I grieve for you, Mother, for the anxiety in your heart during the flight into Egypt.

Everything had gone so well since the birth of your child – no illness, no arrest; Joseph continued to go to his workshop, and you cared for the child, sometimes taking the time simply to sit down and contemplate him. True, you had been busy when those astrologers arrived from the Orient. Like everyone else, they had to eat, and you had to find them a place to stay. At first their visit amused you: they entered bowing low and talked about a star they had seen on their diagram of the heavens, and had followed to find your child. You worried when they told you they had spoken with King Herod about their search. You wondered if one day your family would be singled out by the king's secret services. A strange pain pierced your heart when they asked to see your child and said he was 'born to be king.' It reminded you of the angel's announcement. Different voices seemed to converge deep in your heart, and sometimes, when your child slept, you thought about what they said. The angel, Elizabeth, Zechariah, the shepherds, Simeon, Anna, and now the astrologers, said your child was a king. Did king mean Messiah, the Messiah of the prophecies? With your parents, your family, and all your people you yearned for this Messiah, for the Saviour. The Saviour had never come before. Had he come now? It made you ponder.

But not now! Not now! You have no time to ponder. You have to gather all your belongings, and flee the country because Joseph is convinced that King Herod, in one of his passionate rages, will send out his soldiers to find and kill your child. Joseph, more efficient than you had thought, had taken the first donkey he could find, and now you carefully place your little child in your arms, reluctant to disturb his sleep.

Even on the open road your fears are not dispelled. You are so anxious that you don't see the sheaves in the fields rise up and bow to you, as the astrologers had done. Neither do you see the sun and the moon and eleven stars bow down as your trio advances slowly toward a foreign land. You are too preoccupied with tending your child, with finding some place to rest for the night, even if it be another manger. You plod on, not finding a place to lay your head. The journey is exhausting and all the time you fear that Herod's wild horses will come up behind you, that the soldiers will arrest you with swords and cudgels, and that they will

slaughter your first and only child. But God rides with
you, Mother, God is with us.

I grieve for you, Mother, for the motherly anxiety in
your heart during the flight into Egypt.

(7) Third Sorrow: The Search in the Temple for Jesus

'Son, why have you treated us like this? Your
father and I have been anxiously searching for
you.' 'Why were you searching for me?' he
asked. 'Didn't you know I had to be in my
Father's house?'

Luke 2.48–49

I grieve for you, Mother, for your troubled heart at the
loss of your Jesus.

You had left with half of the population of Nazareth, it
seemed, for Jerusalem. Because you had been a refugee,
you knew what this whole commemoration was about,
more so than the others. So you had to go, with a sheep
from the garden, some hyssop and a few bitter herbs.
Joseph took the unleavened bread, the girdles, the
sandals and the staff. You felt that same strange pain you
had felt before when, as part of the crowd you pondered
upon this upcoming Passover. You didn't understand
why each year the ceremony of the slaughtered sheep
was necessary, and why Passover demanded a victim.
Hadn't you seen enough killing by now? But it was a
tradition.

At the stops along the road, you looked at Jesus piping
songs with other children; they shouted with joy at each
other. In Jerusalem you took Jesus by the hand when you

walked miles and miles to find the family with whom you would stay. Your boy found himself quickly at ease; with other youths he was sitting in the marketplace, among merchants, sheep and some blind people who liked to talk to him. He had told you after a week or so that he knew the whole city, the office of the temple police, the Mount of Olives, the villa of the High Priest and that he had seen Governor Pilate pass by in a gorgeous robe. Of course he was there when on the tenth day your sheep was slaughtered, when you dipped a spray of hyssop in the blood of the animal and put some of it on the lintel and the doorposts of the house where you were staying. Of course he was there at the big barbecue afterwards with all that meat that was left over, the unleavened bread and the herbs. He listened carefully when you explained to him that God had passed over the houses of your people in Egypt, that this Passover had become a memorial and that he had to remember this sacrifice as a sign on his hand and as a cross on his forehead.

There was chaos in Jerusalem when the festival was over. Transportation was bad. All the people from Nazareth had to leave at noon by the Beautiful Gate. You thought Jesus was with his friends in another group. So the whole day you talked with neighbours, dozed off a few times and prepared something for Joseph to eat.

But when you saw a group of children along the road, not seeing Jesus, you began to worry. Suddenly you thought that Jesus could have stayed behind in Jerusalem. You stood up, completely pale, you screamed asking the driver to stop and ran from one to the other, shouting: 'Where is Jesus? Have you seen my Jesus? I've lost Jesus.' Nobody had seen him. Joseph thought that Jesus had perhaps stayed too long with his friends and had missed the departure. There was no choice: you had to return. And it took you three days of suffering, of sleepless nights, of walking and walking in despair before you saw Jesus rising from the temple.

Were those teachers stupid that they hadn't told Jesus to go home? They must have talked him into religious life or a vocation. And from whom had Jesus learned this obstinacy, this recalcitrant behaviour? How did he dare treat his parents like this? But when Jesus came running down the hill towards you, your fears were gone and you cried tears of joy. What had happened? 'Did you not know that I was bound to be in my Father's house?' answered Jesus. You felt a pain in your heart but you took the child in your arms. On the way back, with Jesus leaning against your shoulder, you tried to understand, you reasoned with yourself and you prayed. You prayed to the God of Abraham who finally had not allowed Isaac to be sacrificed, you prayed that nothing of that kind would ever happen to Jesus. Jesus' remark had shaken you. Could it really be true, you thought, that God is his Father, and that Jesus is the Son who would be led like a lamb as a burnt-offering and like a sheep before its shearers?

I grieve for you, Mother, for your troubled and heavy heart at the loss of your Jesus.

(8) Fourth Sorrow: Mary Meets Jesus

> 'Daughters of Jerusalem, do not weep for me; weep for yourselves and for your children. For the time will come when you will say. 'Blessed are the barren women, the wombs that never bore and the breasts that never nursed.'
>
> *Luke 23.28–29*

I grieve for you, Mother, for the distress in your heart at meeting Jesus as he carries his cross.

Again you had come to Jerusalem, this time not only because the festival of Passover was approaching, not only because you wanted to obey the tradition and to spread the blood of your sheep on lintels and doorposts. You had come because your son was in danger. Since that day in the temple twenty years ago you had tried to understand the ministry of your son, all his journeys and encounters, all his anguish and his vocation, all his persecution and his radiance. And now you feel again such pain in your heart, to see Jesus on a donkey descending into Jerusalem, like a sheep willingly entering a den of wolves. For one moment you had thought that the prediction of the angel and the astrologers and the shepherds would come true, and that Jesus would win over his contradictors and lead your people as Shepherd and as King. But too many signs portended defeat and disaster. You feared and you felt in your heart that your son's love would be betrayed, his vocation tested, his body broken, his blood shed. On the road you prayed that an angel from heaven would bring him strength, and you prayed that for once you would not have to give him up.

Upon your arrival, friends told you that a crowd had come to Jesus with swords and cudgels; that he had been led to the High Priest's house, blindfolded and insulted; that he had been brought before the Council of Elders; that he was indicted for blasphemy, subversion and opposition to the Roman Empire; that he had been sent to Pilate, and then to Herod, and then again to Pilate; that the Governor had wanted to be merciful but that the people, enraged and maddened, demanded his death. Your friends said that terrible thing: that Jesus would be crucified, crucified. 'My Jesus, crucified? Innocent, but like a sheep led to be slaughtered? Not guilty, but tortured on a cross with bandits and brigands? His blood on the lintel of a cross? Guiltless but punished, struck, destroyed – my first-born? Did God not see the clots of blood falling to the ground from his hands and from his forehead? Did God not see that this was God's own son in flesh and blood?'

Your friends took you to a place close to Golgotha, and there on the corner of the street you saw him walking with the cross on his back, succumbing under the weight of suffering. All those people separated you from him, all wailing and screaming. You would have run towards him but you couldn't, you couldn't take one single step. You would have preferred that mountains fall on you and cover you. At one moment Jesus turned to you and you looked into his eyes so pure and free; for only a moment they were deeper, deeper than distress. Your womb had born this man, your son, now condemned to death but somehow glorious, somehow fulfilled and victorious. The soldiers pushed him forward, and you stood there incapable of following him. Like a statue you stood there, with your arms wide open as if you wanted to embrace from this moment forth all generations, all peoples and all sorrow – repeating over and over again: 'O God, take pity on me, I have had more than my share of scorn, more than my share of sorrow.'

I grieve for you, Mother, for the deep distress in your heart at meeting Jesus as he carries his cross.

(9) Fifth Sorrow: The Crucifixion

> Near the cross of Jesus stood his mother, his
> mother's sister, Mary the wife of Clopas, and
> Mary of Magdala.
>
> *John 19.25*

I grieve for you, Mother, for the martyrdom which you endured in standing near Jesus in his agony.

It must have been the longest day of your life, a day without end and without respite, a day during which you died yourself so many times. You felt powerless and lifeless when the soldiers crucified Jesus at nine o'clock in the morning. The nails, the blood, his face – you couldn't look at him. Soldiers forbade you to approach too closely to help, to touch your son; terror nailed you to your place; you buried yourself in the arms of your sister and of Mary of Magdala. The morning lasted so long, hopelessly long; the morning was so desolate, irreversibly desolate.

From time to time you uttered some scarcely under-standable words to the other women, asking why, why the soldiers did this, for what crime, how was this possible. But you heard your son, in the prime of his life but now hung on a cross, praying: 'Father, forgive them, they do not know what they are doing.'

There was this other man at Jesus' side, a thief or brigand mean enough to mock at Jesus, as if he did not care about life or death. A man hung and close to death ridiculed Jesus for hanging next to him. Or was it despair that motivated him, was it hope for a miracle, hope that Jesus' prayer would work and that the nails would be hammered out of his hands and feet? Had Jesus not accomplished miracles, one after the other? But you heard Jesus saying: 'I tell you this: today you shall be with me in Paradise.'

At noon darkness fell over the land. Jesus visibly weakened. Each time he looked at you, you felt such pain as if you were pierced to the heart. How can I live without him? you thought. Let me die too, let me die. Let *me* die, not Jesus, you prayed. In the arms of the other women you lamented: 'What will become of me.' But you heard Jesus saying to you: 'Mother.' He called you by your most intimate name; he, the Son, called you, you who had been made mother by the grace of God in the communion of the Holy Spirit. 'Mother,' he said, 'there is your son,' looking at John the disciple. Jesus is your son, Jesus is the fruit of your womb but all his disciples are your sons and daughters. We will take you into our home, we will be with you after this day during which you died so many times. 'John,' Jesus said, 'there is your mother.' You are our mother; all generations will count you blessed; all generations will grieve for you standing near the cross where Jesus hung.

Mother, you wished it was over for Jesus. When you looked upon him, you saw the despair on his face, the struggle he went through. All the three years of his ministry flashed before his eyes, and he was at the end of his strength. And although you stood there, you couldn't help him. And you heard Jesus crying 'Eli, Eli, my God, my God, why hast thou forsaken me?'

If only God would intervene . . . If only God would show mercy and disclose divine might . . . If only God would come to the side of his servant . . . If only God . . . But Jesus cried: 'I thirst.' And you saw that man running towards him, with a sponge soaked in sour wine, on the end of a cane, holding it to his lips. Whatever that man said or for whatever reason he did it, at least he gave Jesus to drink when he was thirsty.

It was almost three o'clock when you heard Jesus saying: 'It is accomplished.' This is better, you thought; it is better that his suffering comes to an end and that finally he can rest. He has given everything, given his life, given his death, given up everything. He has given himself for his friends, and not alone for them but also for the world, for all people, for all future generations. He has done what he could; he has done what he had to do; he has done what he was called to do.

And then there was a loud cry. His last words were: 'Father, into thy hands I commit my spirit.' And he gave up his spirit.

I grieve for you, Mother, for the martyrdom which you endured in standing near Jesus in his agony.

(10) Sixth Sorrow: The Descent From The Cross

> Joseph of Arimathaea bought some linen cloth,
> took down the body, wrapped it in the linen.
>
> *Mark 15.46*

I grieve for you, Mother, for the wounding of your heart at the descent from the cross.

Had you left, exhausted, shattered? I don't see you, Mother, on this strange evening at Golgotha where people gather, swords glisten and men run along with linen sheets, while in the dark three lifeless bodies hang down from crosses. I don't see you, Mother, on this astounding eve of Passover. Or are you there with the other women, Mary of Magdala, Mary the mother of James the younger and of Joseph, Salome and the mother of the sons of Zebedee, united in grief and

trembling? Were you there when soldiers went to finish
the thieves on their crosses and to clean the place for the
solemnity of Passover? You were there when they
crucified my Lord, you were there when they nailed him
to the tree. Were you there when soldiers pierced Jesus'
side with a lance?

Were you there still when that man of means from
Arimathaea came to the place of the Skull, with a written
order from Pilate in his hand, sent away the soldiers and
took Jesus down from the cross? Were you still there
when Nicodemus came by night with more than a
hundredweight of myrrh and aloes in his hands, like the
strangers at Jesus' birth had done? Or had you left,
exhausted, shattered?

Or did you hold the dead body of Jesus in your arms?
Wherever you were, you stayed with him in the
wounding of your heart; you entered with him in the long
silence of the Sabbath; you rested with him in the prayer
of your soul. Wherever you were, you descended with
Jesus – still so close yet already estranged – into the
unknown world of the dead, as far as you could go. But
the dead we cannot keep, they have crossed a river, they
have turned to another light, they are born into another
life. You remain behind, Mother. Remain in our arms.
We will take you into our house, we will give you to eat.
You are alone now. Please live in our love. We will speak
to you about Jesus. He called you 'mother.' Don't you
remember him saying that he was to be born again? that
he was to rise after three days? Come home and stay with
us.

Will a consoler come to you? There is no consolation
yet, because Jesus spoke to you, even this morning
horribly hung on a cross, while now there is silence, only
silence. There is no consolation yet, because the whole

day you could only endure the unendurable, only stand there, only bleed, only die. You are broken, Mother, in your soul and pierced to the heart. Come home and stay with us.

I grieve for you, Mother, for the wounding of your heart at the descent from the cross.

(11) Seventh Sorrow: The Burial of Jesus

> At the place where Jesus was crucified, there was a garden, and in the garden a new tomb in which no one had ever been laid . . . They laid Jesus there.
>
> *John 19.41–42*

I grieve for you, Mother, for the silence in your heart at the burial of Jesus.

The tomb was in the garden, and trees stood around. Joseph and Nicodemus approached, holding either end of a linen sheet in which Jesus was laid. The women held their hands folded, when in the silence of the evening Jesus descended, lower and lower, into a tomb cut out of the rock. There was such stillness in the garden. Joseph and Nicodemus waited for you. You looked at them, and then they placed a stone against the entrance of the tomb.

I grieve for you, Mother, for the silence in your heart at the burial of Jesus.

(12) Giving Up and Giving Over

> 'You still lack one thing. Sell everything you
> have and give to the poor, and you will have
> treasure in heaven. Then come, follow me.'
>
> *Luke 18.22*

Some time ago I needed a retreat, a time of silence and prayer, to confront that part of me that I don't want to give up. During the retreat I stayed in a room in Paris that looked out on a blind wall. I attached a blanket to the window. Darkness is rarely easy but often helps us to find our way.

Abandoning myself is the way I find my identity in God. Maybe it is better to say: renouncing *and* giving over. These inner movements only exist together, hand-in-hand; in the process of growth towards Christ, they are born from each other, and they unfold simultaneously. This is the 'path of virtue,' the right road for me. Any other way would destroy me.

It is dangerous to let the dimension of giving up take over and to concentrate on the loss of what we mistakenly believe to be abundance. Renunciation, taken in itself, isolated, uprooted from its soil, leads to the brink of panic – as if one had to pass through a gloomy valley or a ravine of darkness, the ravine of one's anguished fear of losing ground and of being abandoned. In myself I may feel at first isolated, cut off and plunged into an emptiness in which there is no way out other than to wait until the seed of confidence sprouts again. This remains a repetitive theme in my own existence every time I forget to be attentive to everything that is given to me and in which I am being fulfilled.

But the call to renunciation and to fullness propels me beyond my anxiety towards the light of Christ. Christ the

Risen One has opened this road and calls me to pass this way to God.

Far from letting myself be swallowed up in a swamp of anxiety, I therefore have to jump, to plunge beyond my own emptiness, to take the road in spite of whatever wants to hold me back, focusing on Christ who opens the way and calls me to follow him joyfully.

The way towards renunciation and fullness has to be entered upon audaciously. It is with audacity, generosity and creativity that the risk of surrendering oneself has to be taken.

And if the leap is not possible, if I remain heedless of the call, engulfed by anxiety, then it is time to contemplate – in others, in the unknown of the future, in emptiness and in my self – the hidden Christ.

My weakness needn't lead to self-contempt or to discouragement. I am able to give, I have gifts even in my weakness, I do exist joyfully in other people's existences. Renouncing does not mean dying but ripening towards Christ, living in an abundance of love without retreating into oneself, living warmheartedly and boundlessly.

The Cross was this relinquishment, in the extreme. And we die with Christ. But the Resurrection announces that death was swallowed up and that in love's ascension there is an abundance of life. Growing towards Christ, dying and rising, means renunciation and fullness, together, one begetting the other.

Christ has been fulfilled in his Resurrection. Fulfilled and fulfilling, he now is present in me, hidden in me, until his life becomes mine. It is up to me to become a visible sign of Christ, a bearer of his life. In this maturing everything can be a way for me to advance in my surrender to Christ. There is nothing to fear.

Are you still anxious because you are not able to give

up and to give over, to give yourself as you would like? To fail, even irredeemably? Finally, only Christ is able to give, in and through me. Only God surrenders – in us – to God.

(13) My Vow: Scaffolding For The Unseen

> 'Do you love me more than all else?'
>
> *John 21.15*

When parents die, children strongly experience that they are next in line. Losing your parents means dying yourself a little or at least wrestling with the acceptance of life and future. You left part of you with them. But part of them you take with you, and this part urges you to take up the baton of your own destiny. But before continuing on your way alone, it is good to sit down and to ask: What am I going to do in this void, which reveals the perspective of my own death and confronts me with the unseen? Courage is needed to raise a scaffolding and to start to build the edifice of your vow. This is mine:

Chosen by Christ Jesus – God's self-offering – I want to abandon myself to Christ in all the dimensions of my life.

All the energy which I invest to close my life around myself and to be content – I want to invest in abandoning myself:

surrendering myself to Christ, to the kingdom;

relinquishing the search for myself, this refusal to lose myself, this insistence on the debts I am owed.

I want to let go of my life so that Christ may use it for the sake of the kingdom.

Only by making this self-offering concrete – daringly, radically – in my encounters with others and in the shape of my existence can I become one being with Christ.

The way forward leads from fear to letting go –
limitlessly – to trusting Christ.

This is the adventure and the grace of my life, the
structure of my existence – the vocation to be a reflection
of God's self-offering.

(14) The Downward Ascent

> The curtain of the temple was torn in two from
> top to bottom. The earth shook and the rocks
> split. The tombs broke open and the bodies of
> many holy people who had died were raised to
> life.
>
> *Matthew 27.51–52*

Our 'pilgrimage of reconciliation' has brought us to
Nebraska. On this Friday the cross is laid down on the
floor in the Cathedral of Grand Island, Nebraska.
Tradition, however, demands that there be a sermon,
and it is my turn. So I climb the spiralling stairs of the
pulpit while fighting the feeling of raising myself as a
harpooner in a whaling boat. The silence of the people in
the pews, in the faint evening light, whispers a welcoming sound. This is what is on my mind:

On this very Friday people are dying. Death is there
every day, as a burning wound. So much of our life is
mirrored by the reflections of death. We are blinded and
dazzled by its epiphanies; its long shadows run into the
sunny times of our happiness. Happiness gives only what
it can, in its fugitiveness. The light in someone's eyes
when you entered a room, the whispers you alone could
understand, the cups, ashtrays, flowers, clothes, beds
and books that now seem without any presence, like idle
ruins in a nonsensical desert – you feel as if your own life
were now given over and buried away.

Is our life going downhill, descending into an abyss of annihilation after we have worked so purposefully to build, to gather, to heighten? How many people, advancing in years, are struck by the feeling of having accomplished nothing, of having been nothing, of not having loved enough, of not having even lived at all? Even Jesus, on whom the disciples had projected so many hopes, seemed to become a victim of human decline and death in the same way as everybody else. Handed over to the foreign power, mocked, maltreated, spat upon, flogged and killed – 'they understood nothing of all this; they did not grasp what he was talking about; its meaning was concealed from them.'

But not for long! Jesus was this rabbi they had followed, fascinated; they had left the meshed network of figures, pleasures and guarantees to walk in the footsteps of someone who had gathered disciples to set out for Jerusalem where God would wait for them, bring justice and liberate all people. Jesus was this brother of the poor who with innocence and truth wrote promises of forgiveness in the sand. Jesus was this carpenter who had told them with unmistakable inner authority: 'Before Abraham was, I am.' Jesus was for them all they could hope for from God. Jesus' love never came to an end. It was clear for the disciples that 'the divine nature was his from the first; yet he made himself nothing, assuming the nature of a slave.' Before long, they would recognize Jesus the Christ in his broken body, in the breaking of the bread, in the seal of the promised Holy Spirit.

On this very Friday our life doesn't go downward; our life is a life of ascent. 'There was an earthquake, the rocks split and the graves opened.' In Jerusalem a revolution has taken place. History has reversed itself. The universe has taken another direction. Now, looking back from

Golgotha at Bethlehem, Capernaum, Jericho and the roads to Jerusalem – it becomes clear that Jesus on his pilgrimage reverses the world's pattern. Wherever he goes, those who are below, the humble and the poor, those who suffer, the hungry and the peacemakers, those whose lives seem to go downhill and those who live in the catacombs are up front, walking next to him on humanity's road. 'The arrogant of heart and mind he has put to rout, he has torn imperial powers from their thrones, but the humble have been lifted high. The hungry he has satisfied with good things, the rich sent empty away.' Jesus leads to heaven where we thought hell would be. Jesus the Christ transfigures our darkest desperation into a springtime of hope.

We are invited to experience the risen Christ in us as a pilgrim, accompanying each human being in his or her suffering. Invited to walk with Christ on the road to Emmaeus, in the alleys of Soweto, at Port Authority in New York. We walk to see the light in the eyes of millions of men and women; all the days of our life, we walk with shopping bag ladies and mental patients; we walk with enemies to negotiation tables – yes, we walk together. It is all Christ's pilgrimage, reversing the world's pattern, bringing hope, bringing heaven in the obscurity of death.

In every obscurity Christ in us is the morning star, the horizon spreading its light. Let Christ rise up in us from the obscurity of death to the light of our vocation. Let Christ take over our existence and own whatever belongs to God. So even death will no longer be the fatal end but a birth into that other dimension of the Cross: the fullness of God's love. In our ascent, 'sleeper, awake, rise from the dead, and Christ will shine upon you.'

3

Travelling in the Gospel

Do you really want to live your lives, every moment of your lives, in His Presence? Do you long for Him, crave Him? Do you love His Presence? Does every drop of blood in your body love Him? Does every breath you draw breathe a prayer, a praise to Him? Do you sing and dance within yourselves, as you glory in His love? Have you set yourselves to be His, and *only* His, walking every moment in holy obedience? I know I'm talking like an old-time evangelist. But I can't help that, nor dare I restrain myself and get prim and conventional. . . . Do you want to live in such an amazing divine Presence that life is transformed and transfigured and transmuted into peace?

– Thomas R. Kelly, A Testament of Devotion

(1) Christ Is A Pilgrim

> 'After I have risen, I will go ahead of you into
> Galilee.'
>
> *Mark 14.28*

Christ is a pilgrim on the two-way thoroughfare between
God and every human being. In living, dying and rising
again Christ reveals God – who is offering love but who is
nonetheless rejected. Christ substitutes a 'yes' for
humanity's 'no'. Only Christ responds to God. But by
the 'yes' to God spoken from within the human family,
Christ brings God home to the starting point of the
human pilgrimage and opens a road towards God. Christ
justifies God's truth and repairs humanity's injustice.
Christ reconciles humanity with God and binds them
together, indissolubly. In Christ we respond to God.

Christ is a pilgrim going back and forth between God
and humanity. Christ lives human life and death as a
mystery of offering love so that God may be glorified and
that we may know God. Living and dying in the
perspective of offering love means being filled with the
desire that God be revealed. God raises Christ from
death in order to confirm God's own revelation by
Christ's living and dying and to insist: I am, I am the
life. The risen Christ, really present no longer in flesh but
in the body of the Spirit, lives a resurrected life in us, in
all who recognize God, today for the salvation of all
humanity, tomorrow only in and for God.

Christ is a pilgrim journeying from God to humanity
and from humanity to God. Christ is inseparable from
the human family to whom God's offering of love was
given on the cross and inseparable from God whose
offering of love raises Christ from death. Christ is life,

because in Christ love meets love, no longer mingled with the enmity of rejection.

(2) What Fascinates You in Jesus?

> 'I tell you the truth, God will give you whatever you ask in my name. Until now you have not asked for anything in my name. Ask and you will receive, and your joy will be complete.'
>
> *John 16. 23–24*

What kind of questions do you come across in your travels? a friend asks me. People often tell me that they are unable to influence the world or their church or even themselves. Many suffer from feelings of uselessness. 'Even my own children don't want to go to church.' 'I've tried over and over again to stop but I can't.' 'Rather than to go into politics I want to make some money for myself.' These feelings of uselessness, failure, withdrawal are a complex linked to the overriding importance given to success, efficiency and visible results. By these values we are measured winners or losers. We judge ourselves harshly for not being efficient, even in the spiritual life. Losing is the worst demon. The question I come across is: is this emphasis on efficiency reconcilable with the Gospel? Is efficiency a notion of the Gospel? What is the difference between a successful life and a life that bears fruit? Between the need for visible results and the gift of fruitfulness?

Bearing fruit has to do with roots. The Gospel invites us to bear fruit only by rooting ourselves in Christ. This rootedness is the key. The first question seen from the Gospel is not: what are the results? but: what in Christ is fundamental to me? Not the blossoms but the roots are our responsibility. Whatever will grow out of it will be a gift and whatever will be given will even deepen our roots. 'Set your mind on God's kingdom and God's justice before everything else, and all the rest will come to you as well' (Matthew 6. 33). We are called to be a reflection of Christ. Christians today have to represent something of the ordinary and the extraordinary in the life of Christ, being enabled by the Spirit to incarnate God's love. Of course, we can't reflect Christ's full life, but we can share an outline we have seen, a fragment that we have grasped. Whatever we may have understood, whatever we are most comfortable with, fits us best – the way comfortable clothes fit us – is given to us as the aspect of the life of Christ we are called to represent.

But nothing fits us, nothing penetrates us unless it reaches our inmost suffering. Someone abandoned by his or her parents will be more attentive to and fascinated by Christ as the good shepherd and will be called to become a good shepherd to others. Someone who has not been loved in the right way will be grasped by Christ's trust in the love of God and will be called to become a person of trust. A person's particular gift of faith may be held back deep within his or her heart: it needs to rise, to well up from obscurity towards clear awareness.

We are also called to see a reflection of Christ in every person. What is the worth, the efficiency of a handicapped person? Are handicapped children a failure by worldly standards? Friends of mine made a marvellous film about the handicapped but some TV stations turned them down because 'viewers don't like to look at failures.' Why is the unfortunate person considered a loser? Or is he or she not? Isn't the handicapped child teaching us something about God?

If we are called to bear fruit by being rooted more and more totally in Christ, then why? Fruit for what? For a new humanity, for a future for all. The church is the anticipation of that future, of people belonging together, renewing the face of the earth, reconciling and peace-making. If, personally and collectively, we want to bear fruit, our effort will be to allow Christ to rise up in us to meet the deepest desires and expectations of the human family, to emerge from us in his fullness so that God can be recognized.

Through the Gospel runs this paradoxical thread: being active but resting in God. We have to work so that Christ is doing it; if we can't do it in spite of all our efforts, Christ will accomplish it. Don't look at the results you obtain but abandon yourself to God's love. Trust that in distress and suffering all of human life has a meaning of salvation and that God will more and more be all in all.

So the question I really hear is: who are we in Christ? And even further back: what has fascinated me in Jesus? This is the right question, the question that should be asked; all others are secondary. Later on we will ask ourselves: How can we change our way of looking at people and events, not with competition or anxiety which cuts us off, but with a way of looking that is filled with trust in God's fruitfulness for every human being?

Does this lead us to passivity, or could it lead to commitment to a new future for all? Rooted in the risen Christ, what and where are our priorities?

What is it about Jesus as he is portrayed in the Gospel (not the transcendent Christ, so easily confused with our own projections) that intrigues you, fascinates, disturbs, puzzles you? It might be something he did, something he said, or it may be something characteristic of his personality. Think about the first thing that comes to mind. Why did that particular thought arise? It is a way of discovering what is going on between God and us because Jesus is the horizon of our encounter with God, the horizon of revelation. Is your fascination the continual awareness of God in Jesus? Is it Jesus' capacity to welcome odd sorts of people? Whenever anybody vividly thinks of herself or imagines himself over against Jesus, the part of them that is living the death and resurrection of Jesus is touched. Burdens and suffering are a part of that. The reason we are fascinated by a particular story of Jesus has something to do with the story of our own life or of our own people. God is approaching us and drawing us into his mystery; the way we react to the image of Jesus is a clue to the way God is approaching us in our life, be it in some previous psychological experience, or more directly, in some challenge or in some demand coming to our freedom.

As soon as you have found Christ's revelation in yourself, life unfolds: faith and roots, commitment and wings, love and blossoms.

(3) A Summer Above The City

> 'I tell you the truth, if you have faith as small as
> a mustard seed, you can say to this mountain,
> "move from here to there" and it will move.'
> *Matthew 17.20*

A man came to see us one day on 48th Street, unannounced, at five o'clock in the afternoon. We were just sitting by ourselves around the table. Having walked up the hundred stairs to the fifth floor in a hurry, the tall and corpulent man sat down out of breath. We are used to letting visitors rest for a while and coming to themselves before starting the conversation. The man's blue eyes gradually ceased their constant movement. He had read, he said, the rule of our Community, a long time ago, in a period of his life in which he drank very heavily. Our rule had been one of the parts of his decision to quit his addiction. He had come to visit us because being very wealthy, he wanted to offer us his property on the Hudson, two hours from New York City. He told us that from the highest point of the property one could see Manhattan's skyscrapers in the distance. We were perplexed. It is part of our vocation not to own any property whatsoever, and we refuse gifts, donations, wills and inheritances. We want to earn our living ourselves without being dependent on benefactors. On the other hand, was this man's gesture not an invitation at least to undertake something together?

To make a long story short, we decided to spend one summer on his property and to welcome young adults for prayer and retreat. We asked the owner and his family to be there and to take part, together with us, in the event. With this decision the man's generosity was honoured but his personal involvement was also implied. By the end of the summer the owner had found a group of anti-alcoholics to whom he donated his property. For us this place offered a unique possibility to invite young people and some older people whom we could not welcome on 48th Street because of the limitations of our apartment. They came for a week-long retreat: each week a different group arrived. We improvised some outdoor showers, transformed a living room with walls of glass into an intimate chapel, turned the vinery into a meeting room, and moved in for the duration of an alternately hot and rainy summer.

With the participants we built a small community praying together three times a day, taking meals together on a patio, and sharing everything we had. Sometimes we went to the local church down the hill, taking part in liturgies and local groups in order not to lose contact with the down-to-earth reality of the Church. On our hill we could have lived somewhere between heaven and earth!

The theme we wanted to explore was the discovery of the face of Christ in us. Which face of Christ challenges me the most? Which face of Christ inspires me, is the most accessible to me, or questions me? Each morning, therefore, we studied one event in Jesus' life as depicted in the Gospel, and every evening each one of us spoke about his or her personal discovery of Christ. We compared and contrasted our own images of Jesus with those of the others and those of the Gospel: glimmerings of understanding that, pieced together, form an inner portrait of Jesus in our own life. The time between our meetings was used for personal meditation on the Gospel studied together. We were invited to use our imagination and to place ourselves in that Gospel, with our reactions of joy, anxiety and amazement while looking at Jesus' gestures and listening to Jesus' words.

In a first meeting participants expressed spontaneously the face of Jesus as they saw it reflected in their own experiences. Jesus was seen as the prophet who sets free and who challenges us to break out of our limitations, or as the servant and man of sorrows, as the master whom one can really trust or as the Lord present in my self, the source and strength of my life. But how can we translate his call in the concrete choices we have to make, in our relationships, in our plans for the future? Where does he lead us, into which unknown?

Together we saw Jesus transfigured on the mountain;

at one moment we saw nothing but Jesus and the disciples. We felt like the disciples, not knowing what was going on and fearing, and we too wanted to settle down within this glory far from the disfigured world. Jesus transcends our images of him, his light shines out in the fulfilment of human longing, his voice opens up the way of our own transfiguration in the labyrinths through which we wander.

Together we saw Jesus with the adulterous woman; at one moment we saw nothing but ourselves waiting for a judgement. We felt like the men who preferred to leave the scene, ashamed of ourselves. We tried to decipher what Jesus wrote in the sand. Jesus looks upon us with trust; his forgiveness instils joy and gladness into us; his writing in the sand teaches us more than a thousand words.

Together we saw Jesus at the Last Supper; at one moment we saw nothing but Jesus kneeling down at the feet of his friends. We felt shocked like the disciples, not knowing how to behave in this reversal of roles and we too wanted to wash away our jealousy and our judgements, our competition and our criticism. Jesus serves, and shows us the way of love; his voice whispers in our ears the truth about ourselves; we will never understand all of the immense implications of this simple gesture at the Last Supper.

Together we contemplated the risen Jesus. Unseen, hidden – where can we hear his voice, his presence if not with the eyes of love? Only love opens our eyes, only love enables us to recognize the living Christ, hidden at the heart of every suffering, every questioning and striving, every longing and in the least audible sighs.

At the end of the week we asked ourselves what links exist between the face of Christ we discover in ourselves, and our vocation. The face of Christ that fascinates us indicates the gift we receive and the road we should follow to share this face, this gesture and these words around us. We are in charge of, we are responsible for, this face that has been born in us, and we are called to reflect this very face wherever we go.

But then we understand that on our own we cannot express every facet of Christ. His fullness can only be grasped in the communion of the whole Church. There we correct, complete, unite each other's perceptions; there we stand before the face of the Other, greater than our heart. Your face remains ever open, o Risen from the dead.

(4) The Listener

> 'The kingdom of heaven is like treasure hidden
> in a field. When a man found it, he hid it again,
> and then in his joy went and sold all he had and
> bought that field.'
>
> *Matthew 13.44*

Who has listened to you in the past year? Do you recall anybody you wanted to speak to and who listened? Somebody who revealed you to yourself, who did not judge you and in whose eyes you saw acceptance and love? Many young people especially have the bitter experience of nobody listening to them. So fragmented are our minds, so drowned in the modern tumult our voices, and so deafened our ears that we often hardly see, hear, feel the presence of the one who is at our side. As a result, human relationships and the value of the other have become superficial and cheap.

I asked a young man, married and successful, apparently at ease with himself but on fire for God, what fascinated him in Jesus. He answered: 'The Listener, his total and undivided presence.' Reading the Gospel, he is drawn to the passages where Jesus speaks directly, for instance 'Do you love me?' and 'You, follow me.' The depth, the intensity of this presence almost frightens him. Why? Because it is the Son of God who speaks, looks at, turns to *you*; because it is impossible to avoid, to dilute, to escape from such a love. 'What, do you look at me this very moment, you my Lord and my God?'

To receive the undivided attention of a man or a woman whose being is not fragmented, the attention of somebody who is totally there and who listens to us without inner division, is almost a miracle. It is so new. A person who, at any moment, can be with us simply and totally, disarms us, warms us and reaffirms the infinite importance of each one of us. This patient way of looking, this inviting attitude, these eyes encouraging us or this smile that creates trust and already knows everything are characteristic of Christ. Only the person who lives from deep sources and whose life is a long dialogue with God is capable of such attentiveness: 'I am here, I am listening to you. Speak if you want.' This is the way God turns to us when we are in silence, in contemplative waiting, in prayer: 'I am here, with you. Remain anchored in our encounter. We have all eternity before us.'

The young man thinks of Jesus on earth talking to Zaccheus in his tree, turning to Nathanael, answering John's question in the Cenacle with the intimacy of a whispering voice. For a moment everything stops because the Son of God looks upon them, they hear his voice, and he is totally there and invites them to live this present moment with him. His presence embraces them. Whenever their encounter lasts, it is as though eternity has made them forget the time. Never has one human being been so present to another. Never has a human encounter borne such compassion. What a lesson for those of us who are sometimes scarcely able to listen!

For the young man this is a lesson of love. Christ, who gave us the commandment to love, also shows us how to listen. How deeply do we hunger and thirst in our loud society to be listened to and to be appreciated as irreplaceable people! To us, for whom time has become a busy schedule and work nothing but money and power, Jesus offers an endless presence, unconditionally: 'I am there, with you, forever.'

(5) 'My, Oh My': The Awe of a Confessor

> 'Come to me, all you who are weary and burdened, and I will give you rest. . . . For my yoke is easy and my burden is light.'
>
> *Matthew 11.28–30*

We were maybe two hundred people gathered for the Eucharist in a convent in Burlingame, California. I had come late and had to sit in one of the last pews. The priest was preaching about the healing of the leper.

When listening to a sermon, you first have to come to grips with the preacher. Who is this who preaches to us? You want to feel at ease with the preacher's personality before you decide to become vulnerable to the message. I found him very intense, as if he had to go a long way in reaching out from his introverted depths to this Californian surface. He looked like a modern Atlas doomed to support the whole earth on his shoulders. He almost excused himself for preaching. And then his frailty and shy gentleness came through. His emphatic way of speaking had tired him. He could no longer find the words to express his empathy with the world. One expression came back as a recurring staccato: 'My, oh my.' His grieving over the world reminded me of David's lament over Absalom 'My son, my son, my son.' It must have launched me into a reverie because I had to return from faraway wanderings when I heard the priest pronouncing my name and asking me to share my concerns with the congregation.

After the celebration I went to his room. Like Jesus coming out of the synagogue and visiting with Peter's mother-in-law, he uses a room nearby to escape and to recharge his battery. Why this intensity? In his own words, 'all my life, and in particular in my preaching, I have been compensating for my personal inadequacy. The book of the Bible has never belonged to me. Even after thirty-seven years of priesthood, I still can't open up and proclaim the Scriptures.'

'Come on,' I say, 'one doesn't preach with words and clever comments but with life and love. Our example should be Saint John, who at the end of his life only repeated again and again: love one another.'

But there is another side to his feeling of inadequacy. When he is at the altar, he is acutely aware of his human weakness because 'it is awesome to stand there with the living Jesus.' Christ is for him the High Priest who lives to make intercession before the Father and who gives his death and resurrection as a constant offering to the Father. 'My, oh my, my, my, all that goes through you during the celebration.' On the other hand, he feels that Christ identifies with the agony and passion in the world, the suffering of the outcasts, the leprosy of our time. 'There is so much of it and it is so awful.' 'For instance in the history of the leper, Jesus identifies with this man and suffers with him. This falls as a burden on me. How do we live with the poor?'

In former days he was more familiar with the omnipotent Christ, faraway, which led to a certain aloofness, removing his priesthood from the reality of struggle and anxiety. But now he sees Jesus as one of us, suffering, discovering deeper dimensions in his vocation, constantly going to God, asking to be enlightened, a man like us. He struggled with the temptation to be relevant, to be able to speak to all of the people, to say something that would really impress them. Earlier the church had the tendency to remain linked to strength, power, and wealth. Unfortunately, the mark is still very much on the church. 'But what a hope there is when the church – leadership, priests and all its members – become like the people in their poverty and weakness. There lies the authority of Jesus. He suffers with the poor; he didn't cling to his Godhead; he surrenders himself, he comes down to us, and walks with us. And isn't that what love is?'

Now it is my turn to say 'My, oh my'; I am awed to rediscover the holiness of the priesthood. A scholar, a learned priest, a brilliant preacher? His ministry as confessor keeps him alive. There lies his consolation. He is filled with the awareness of how good and how holy people are. And so he can stand at the altar with the living Jesus.

Like all holy people, he sees holiness all over the place. He is intense but he smiles, too; he fights but he is filled with peace. He looks like arched Atlas, but he is simply one of the humble hearted honoured with the yoke of

Jesus' ministry. To our worldly world he may appear a bit wooden, but the reason is that he suffers with Christ the sufferings of humanity.

(6) A Keynote Speaker's Question

> At midnight the cry rang out: 'Here's the bridegroom! Come out to meet him!'
>
> *Matthew 25.6*

'Who is this God we have to endure?' I read on the poster behind the church official's seat. I know from myself how much suspicion and scepticism can insinuate themselves into the freshness of faith we started out with. As we get older, there is a danger of becoming infatuated with ourselves to the point that God burdens us. The need to affirm ourselves imperceptibly alters the identity entrusted to us: we become managers instead of fools for Christ, philanthropists instead of saints, PRs instead of disciples, and fund-raisers instead of signs of contradiction. At every age we need a bath of youthfulness.

At the Mid-America youth ministry conference on the grounds of Notre Dame University nine hundred young people, sixteen to eighteen years old, are gathered together in the big athletic arena, somewhat reorganized for the event. On the platform stands a man from Louisiana who has the task of breaking the ice and warming the young people up. He works very hard on his guitar, jumps around and commands his crowd masterfully. Like a Prince of Serendip he makes us discover our neighbour by pinching their cheeks, by playing patty-cake, by giving them hugs and by telling each other who has influenced us in a very personal way. As soon as the attention grows, the speaker drops some facts about runaways, some statistics about drug-addicted youth. From behind this show-biz style there emerges a perfectly coherent keynote talk.

In the last part of his talk, while playing the guitar that hangs across his chest like a bandolier, he asks the excited young people to think about the question, 'Who is Jesus for us?' Let some of you, he asks, stand up and one by one say in one sentence how you see Jesus. Perhaps the ice is not completely broken or the question is a hard one: it takes some time before the first dares to rise. But then several others inundate us with a fountain of faith:

> Jesus is the inspiration!
> Jesus, I want to live 4 U!
> You bring feeling to my life!
> We are friend to friend!
> Jesus is all I need!
> You give my life direction!
> He's really got a hold on me!
> I've got to take a little time for Jesus!
> You make everything so clear!
> Nobody loves me like Jesus does!
> Jesus saves me from myself!
> I just want to say I love you!
> I put my life in your hands!
> Coz I feel so secure when we're together!
> I want you with me from today until the end of time!
> For them faith is a love story. Could it be the same for me?

(7) 'It Is I! Don't Be Afraid'

> About the fourth watch of the night he went out to them, walking on the lake. . . . They all saw him and were terrified. Immediately he spoke to them, and said, 'Take courage! It is I! Don't be afraid.'
>
> *Mark 6.48–50*

In moments of solitude and anguish we talk to ourselves in an unconscious language – as we do sometimes in love or in prayer. This is what I heard myself say one day: You are not alone, little child, when your mother goes away, when your mother is not home. You are not alone, little child, when your father cries out in pain, when your father walks alone. You are not alone, little boy, when your friends let you down, when your friends stir you up. You are not alone, little boy, when no one understands you, when no one breaks the ice. You are not alone, dear friend, when you see no future, when you see no love. You are not alone, dear friend, when you have no money, when you find no work. You are not alone, man, when no business comes along, when no woman smiles at you. You are not alone, man, when you run out of luck, when you lose your chance. You are not alone, man, when you slam the door, when you feel so lonely. You are not alone, man, when your friends do better, when your friends are only good for a laugh. You are not alone, father, when you see the years go by, when you see yourself withdraw. You are not alone, father, when you see the day darkening, when you see the night falling.

You are not alone, mother, when you stand at the tomb, when you return to an empty home. You are not alone, mother, when you lie alone in bed, when you awaken in the night. You are not alone, woman, when the days have no meaning, when you are shut in at home. You are not alone, woman, when your children leave the house, when your husband stays away. You are not alone, woman, when your life is confined, when your dreams have to shrink. You are not alone, woman, when you can't accept yourself, when you can't trust yourself. You are not alone, dear friend, when you build up your life, when you start to love. You are not alone, dear friend, when you feel so down, when you suffer from life. You are not alone, little girl, when you run to your room, when you cannot explain. You are not alone, little girl, when your heart hurts so bad, when your heart beats so hard. You are not alone, little child, when your father is so sad, when your father doesn't talk. You are not alone, little child, when your mother closes her eyes, when your mother says goodbye.

(8) The Forgotten Fresco of a White Horse

> 'Look, Master, what huge stones! What fine buildings!' Jesus said to him, 'You see these magnificent buildings? Not one stone will be left upon another; all will be thrown down.'
>
> *Mark 13.1–2*

The rushing 'El' sounds like a carriage pulled by wild horses crashing into a wall of glass. Masses of tall towers escorted the elevated train out of the 'Magnificent Mile' into Chicago's South Loop where everything falls apart. Every city has one such area, untouched by the city planners, used as a dumping ground for whatever is undesirable in the organized world.

I'm looking for a rarely used chapel, hidden in this shabby part of town, where once I was surprised to find a startling modern fresco. It is in a building which houses an agency for undocumented aliens. A foreign-looking man, dozens of keys jingling on his belt, leads me down staircase after staircase to an underground world of corridors where even the screeching noise of the elevated train can't penetrate. Suddenly I'm faced by a life-size figure and a white horse, on the wall of this catacomb.

Canvas murals on the side walls of the chapel symbolize the birth of light. A back wall mural portrays the creation of the universe. Between here and there darkness reigns. Dark colours dominate the canvases. Hospitals, factories, plantations, slums, prisons and cemeteries are twisted into crosses: a history of humanity seen through the eyes of the oppressed.

But before me, the image of Christ and the horse, flanked by a star, an angel and an empty crib on one side and by a rising sun, an angel and an empty tomb on the other side, lights the whole scene. No sun, no moon shines on the city. This apocalyptic rider is turned towards me, his right arm raised in benediction. His hand shows an open wound. A bar of light streams over it and embraces the wounds in his side. The bar of light extends outward to eclipse the sun, turned black, and the moon which has become blood-red.

A vision forgotten by the rulers of the world? A fresco of our future dumped in the catacombs of the fine buildings which make up our city? Heaven is imprisoned – when will it burst out? When will its light penetrate all the surrounding darkness? When will the stones of the world's foundations be thrown down? Below the horse and rider, an angel stoops to strike a rock from which water – living water – streams over the new city of Jerusalem.

There will be Heaven for the undocumented aliens. There will be Heaven for those who have no family and no friends. There will be Heaven for farmers and economists, factory workers and politicians, the unemployed and business people. There will be Heaven for diplomats, lawyers and students. There will be Heaven for missionaries, foster families, teachers, physicians, street-workers and parents. There will be Heaven for children, for the simple-minded, for the handicapped. There will be Heaven for peace-makers, for people who are persecuted for justice, who defend the poor, risking their lives. There will be Heaven for you when they insult you and persecute you, when society rejects you. Heaven . . .

(9) How The Poor Belong

> Jesus looked around and said to his disciples, 'How hard it is for the rich to enter the kingdom of God!' The disciples were amazed at his words. But Jesus said again, 'Children, how hard it is to enter the kingdom of God!'
>
> *Mark 10.23–24*

Salvation is the key to the faith of believers and churches in many denominations. It is the central theme of their hymns and sermons. It is quite particularly the way the poor belong. You long for salvation only when you need it. Those who know that they are poor – materially, spiritually, emotionally, intellectually – evidently long most of all for salvation. Does this mean idealizing the poor? Do my neighbours in New York go to church? No, but wherever poor people do go, the churches become lively with prayers, pilgrimages, singing and longing. In order to discover salvation, you have to be poor, you must recognize your own poverty.

Some people object that this type of fundamental Christianity is only a beginning stage, a primitive phase of self-centredness. They feel that these Christians need to go beyond the personal experience of salvation in order to realize that there is something missing: the depth and the richness of Church history, the awareness of being part of a community of people over time and the realization of a responsibility for the rest of the world. We would like the others to join us in that place we have reached. We would like the others to resemble us, and we invite a poor man to our panels about the politics of food and hunger in celebration of people's struggles all over the world, or a shopping-bag lady to do zazen in a meditation group. But there are different gifts, different emphases. And salvation is the beatitude of the poor. Don't take away the only richness they have!

We pinpoint the intellectual insufficiencies in the faith of believers and churches where salvation is the key. We would do better to espouse their poverty, becoming their sisters and brothers. How? Live with the poor! Only if we live ourselves as poor among the poor, will we be able, looking through their eyes, to perceive what salvation means and to sense how close the Gospel is to them.

But then we will no longer use the term 'poor' as if we were not concerned. The word will hurt us. Our life will have become woven into the lives of the others, discovering their human riches to the point that we will no longer believe that they are poor. We will say: it is not hopeless to be homeless and penniless; these things can be remedied; it is not degrading to be as poor as we are; it is possible to work beyond that; there will always be something higher we can witness to together: God is good! God is our Saviour!

(10) How To Pray in America

'This is how you should pray:
"Our Father . . .".'

Matthew 6.9

In a parish in New York the Hispanics have to pray in the basement so that 'the Americans' can have their Mass in English. I find that a shame. In the Lord's prayer, who does 'our' include? Is it only our club, our class, people who speak our language? Is it only the well-to-do? If the 'our' refers to Americans, we can then ask which Americans? Anglo-Americans? Hispanics? Would our prayer and church life not become much richer and more real if it opened out in an inclusive way? Are you horrified in advance because of the possible conflicts and controversies that could arise as consequences of a common prayer? Do you fear that the inclusion of the others would lead to an assault on the status quo, on the system in which the rich and the poor don't socialize, on our world in which the dominators and the dominated slash their way through as in a jungle?

The question has many ramifications. If God is not only the God of one nation but of all humanity, shouldn't we, imitating this love, find ways to express our common belonging, and first of all in our prayer? The Hispanics are neighbours in the same area, but what about Latin America? If the 'our' in the Lord's prayer refers to Americans, we can then ask: North Americans? Latin Americans? South Americans? They all belong to this part of the world called America. To Latin and South Americans it amounts almost to chauvinism that the people of the United States have no other word for themselves than America. Shouldn't our prayer, whenever it speaks of Americans, include the whole continent, North and South, and not just the United States? Do Latin Americans feel this unity of the Americans? No, they feel animosity, not unity. Latin Americans feel that oppression comes from the North. Theologians in those countries, however, emphasize that these conflicts are only temporary. These theologians express a Utopian view according to which people eventually will join together in a new community. So even if we find ourselves oppressed or in the situation of oppressors by the very fact that we live in one or the other part of America, the Kingdom is for both. The Kingdom is not only for those who are now oppressed, it is also for the oppressors.

How do you build that into a prayer? Could this lead to an intention of prayer? Where is God calling us and speaking to us? We are called to turn to God. Or have we turned away? To the degree that our love is narrow and restricted we can pray that walls fall down, that we turn to those we have turned our backs on, that we turn around to open up what had been closed. Obviously, we lack this openness politically: each country has its 'truth,' and clings to it. All are called to a conversion, and then to perpetual conversion. The ones who simply by belonging to a wealthy and proud country are implicated in political, economic and cultural oppression can pray for their own conversion and change, for more openness towards the persons they are oppressing. The ones who see themselves as oppressed can pray that their hearts be not hardened against those whom they see as their oppressors, and that they may keep an open attitude too. But opening out should not be directed to a dialectic process of an exchange of places between the dominators and the dominated or to the perpetual opposition of turning against each other. The aim is to turn together towards the future and to build that future together. When we burst out of our enclosures, we become ready to build together the Kingdom in which God becomes manifest.

Enrique Dussel, a Latin American philosopher, speaks of a conversion moment, the moment in which we break out of our system of 'what is.' You look at a situation and you find people in that situation who are not partaking in the benefits, who are deprived or are lacking in some way. They will stand up and say: Look, we are not sharing with you. That is the moment to reach out and to include them. Opening out, enlarging our boundaries means a break that always modifies our system and our world.

Who does 'our' include for Americans? In ancient times, all non-Greeks were considered barbarians. In the Middle Ages, Christianity was the centre of the world. In the sixteenth century, people asked whether or not Indians had souls. Can we find ways to manifest to ourselves that 'our' includes all humanity, the Hispanics, the Latin and South Americans, the oppressed and the poor? Of course, we can escape by praying for humanity and neglecting our brother or sister next door, allowing for instance the scandal of poverty to continue in a society of plenty. Or we can become so wrapped up in our next-door neighbour and so worn out in the local soup-kitchen that we never remember that there are other people, other nations, other continents beyond. All these others are necessary for our growth towards the kingdom of Heaven.

We are billions of people, all loved by God; let's talk together. We are all unique, people, nations and continents; let's pray together.

(11) Another Spring

<blockquote>

'You travel over land and sea to win a single convert, and when one person becomes one, you make the convert twice as much a child of hell as you are.'

Matthew 23.15

</blockquote>

'The best analogy,' says an Evangelical observer of the life of the churches in the Northern hemisphere, 'is perhaps a southwestern desert landscape. All around us are *arroyos*, the empty gullies dug by floods from the spring rains, and the great river of institutional Christianity into which they lead is now an extensive mud flat with a thin ribbon of living water wandering through the centre, almost hidden from view. But it requires only another spring for the gullies to fill again and the river to flow full to its banks.'

The 25,000 denominations of Christendom today bear witness to the Church's extraordinary following. One can scarcely imagine the sacrifices of former generations sending their sons and daughters into the jungles of the world to propagate the Gospel. Often they died soon after their arrival. Examples abound, especially in the Third World. But even in Lousiana, now perfectly integrated into the affluent American society, malaria and yellow fever at the end of the last century made victims of priests twenty-seven or twenty-eight years old. Bishops would obtain them from all over the world, but very soon they were wiped out because of all the adverse conditions. They gave their lives, and the Gospel sprouted. But the young churches were the replicas of their parent churches across the ocean, inheriting the battle for souls. All European divisions were exported together with mirrors, guns and bottles. And today groups and sects split apart in such great numbers that unity among Christians has become a Utopian concept. The evening sky in a city like Seoul is illuminated by neon crosses towering above newly installed churches, all divided, all in competition, all the fruit of divorces in the Christian family. What a responsibility we have for the 25,000 denominations of Christendom!

In the meantime we discover that we in the northern hemisphere have become a mission field. Our own churches are not able to find each other in a spirit of reconciliation. Even our personal faith has become a desert because of the influx of agnosticism and cultural conformity.

Where will our healing come from? Will the young churches one day be willing to heal their mother churches, either moribund or caught up in self-defence? Will they help us one day to live out prayer and justice, faith and peace? As I walked through New Bell, the all-African neighbourhood of Douala in Cameroun, people came out of their shacks, threw up their hands and said 'Thank you, Sir!' as if, colonized in their souls, they wanted to thank the white master for coming back again. Will the same people walk one day in our street and evangelize us in our desert? 'It requires only another spring for the gullies to fill again.' It requires only the living water of the Gospel for the river of Christianity to flow full to its banks.

(12) Doodling During Duties

> 'Therefore, if you are offering your gift at the altar and there remember that your brother or sister has something against you, leave your gift there in front of the altar. First go and be reconciled to your brother; then come and offer your gift.'
>
> *Matthew 5.23–24*

I am not the only one who doodles during long church meetings. Some speakers are long and tedious. In ecumenical meetings with representatives of different denominations, people talk and talk. But solutions are slow to come and mentalities not eager to change. So doodling is a way of dreaming up, off the record, worthwhile steps to be taken. But are they realistic? Here are two of my most recent doodles. I hope they shock you as much as they would have shocked the ecumenists around the table who thought that I was taking notes of what they said.

Chambersburg, Penn. – The Evangelicals decided to buy a 'pension' in Rome, not far from the North American College. The aim is to have some of their people always present in Rome. They intend to use their time in Rome for prayer in the catacombs, for pilgrimages from one basilica to another and for meditation upon the major concerns in the Holy Father's addresses. They plan to check in at the main Vatican offices. Those among them who in an earlier period spoke about Rome as Babylon – or worse – have recognized the historical conditions that centuries ago determined that kind of blind opposition to a ministry that has become more and more visibly a ministry of reconciliation for Christians and non-Christians alike.

The Evangelicals explained that they had been amazed themselves about their capacity, not only as individuals but as a body, to retrace their steps, deliberately to take a road that was earlier refused or unrecognized. They have not lost their identity; it is part of their identity, they say, to be able to affirm: now it is time to suffer with, to search with those we forsook and left alone in the past. We don't want to wait until the church is perfect; we are called to live at its heart, to put our shoulders to the wheel of its mission, to be fully part of it and to bring in our own gifts. Our forefathers acted differently. It is not true, however, that being faithful to them means repeating their invectives, accusations and suspicions; it means, on the contrary, re-enacting their obedience, re-inventing attitudes of taking part in the creation of the church by reconciling ourselves with Rome. We repent of the fact that our ancestors ever accused Rome, and the Pope in particular, of being the 'Antichrist.' We turn away from the sin – we who know because of our evangelical background what sin is – of that terrible accusation. We embrace the cross of Christ, and we commit ourselves to the search for reconciliation.

South Bend, Ind. – Somehow this bishop had found a system to get rid of all the management tasks that in the past he had taken to be the core of his ministry. He used to sign checks, to instruct his staff, to fly to Washington, to preside over breakfasts, lunches and dinners, and to give interviews. Priority number one: fund raising. He knew of course that hundreds of priests and millions of lay people who were living all around him had a grievance against him. But he couldn't get out of the vice of all these administrative duties.

One day, reflecting in the plane upon the superhuman duties he had to fulfil day after day, he suddenly became sad recognizing that he didn't struggle enough with his own priests; he blushed at the thought that they too gave in to all the managerial demands and to the worldly conformity this presupposed. Then he remembered the emblem on his coat-of-arms, with the Bible text: 'Feed my sheep.'·

On his arrival at the airport he still repeated the now-classic jokes that were part of his repertory, he still smiled through his sleepy eyes at the fellow diners who used him as an ecclesiastical alibi for their pleasures and dealings. But since that day he has remained after Mass in the cathedral to talk with people. The custodians have had a hard time adapting themselves to this new style. He spends one morning each week with the other church leaders for a morning of contemplation. And he has made this decision: from nine to five he visits with priests, doormen, young people and girls on the street corners he encounters going from one parish to the next. For the people he has become a friend who in times of need puts his arm around their shoulder.

I remember an interview with the bishop by a reporter of the local newspaper. The reporter wondered if the bishop's new style would not become detrimental to the financial soundness of the church. So he asked him: 'How do you support yourself?' The bishop told him that the church had renounced any fund-raising effort that would imply a compromise with the powerful. He admitted that it was extremely hard to draw a clear line. At least in some situations, he said, it had become evident that accepting money would have meant a trade-off for silence about national policies. Secondly, he found it important that the church and the people themselves put a new emphasis on tithing on the one hand and sharing on the other. 'When we are lively communities, when we are intent on Christ's invitation to follow him, we will not be in need, even with only five dollars and two nickels in a parish of three thousand souls.'

(13) A Call To Gather

> 'How often I have longed to gather your
> children together, as a hen gathers her chicks
> under her wings, but you were not willing.'
>
> *Matthew 23.37*

'If I can unite *in myself*,' wrote Thomas Merton, 'the thought and the devotion of Eastern and Western Christendom, the Greek and the Latin Fathers, the Russians with the Spanish mystics, I can prepare in myself the reunion of divided Christians. From that secret and unspoken unity in myself can eventually come a visible and manifest unity of all Christians.'

If I can unite in myself tradition and audacity, struggle for justice and hunger for prayer, I can prepare in myself the reunion of divided Christians. If I can unite in myself the silence of the Quakers with the glossolalia of the Charismatics, the preaching of the Black Baptists and the evensong of the Episcopalians, the Mass of the Catholics and the Spirit within those who are persecuted because of their faith, I can prepare in myself the reunion of divided Christians. If I discover hope not only in those I happen to like, but also learn to probe beyond the affinity-barrier – that perennial middle wall of partition in the Church, if I see hope where the cynic misses it and as the truest of realists learn to see that the same seed of hope requires a vast range of soil-types to produce its finest flowering, I can prepare in myself the reunion of divided Christians. If I weave together the love of truth and the truth of love, I can prepare in myself the reunion of divided Christians.

I may speak in tongues of every prayer group, I may sign every petition against torture in the world, but if I do not search for visible reconciliation, forgiveness and love among Christians, I put the cart before the horse. I may have the gift of theological insight, and find every lost key to the Gospel in the computer age; I may have the conviction that faith expresses itself in spirituality, that discipleship means witnessing, that conversion is the only salvation, that Christianity consists of service to the poor, that our confession of faith today must be the defence of human rights, that obedience to the Gospel leads to mission, that to be born again is the renewal we need; but if I don't love the whole Body of Christ, I am nothing. I may dole out all I possess and give to the poor, or even give my whole life, but if I don't love the Body of Christ in all its members, I am none the better.

We belong together as a brood cared for by the same mother. We belong together as a flock of sheep called together by one shepherd. We belong together to God's family. All of us are loved. All of us are called. All of us are forgiven, again and again. Would we not let the Spirit unite us all?

(14) Travelling in the Gospel

> As they were walking along the road a man said to him, 'I will follow you wherever you go.' Jesus replied, 'Foxes have holes and birds of the air have nests, but the Son of Man has no place to lay his head.'
>
> *Luke 9.57–58*

Another brother and I, on our way to Orange County where we had to lead meetings and retreats, were stuck in San Francisco, having missed a plane. Because we were one day too early anyhow, we decided to take the day off to stroll the streets. Chicago, where we came from, work-oriented as it is, had kept us busy. Chicago is a pragmatic town where hard work and honest labour count. Only Sunday afternoon is an oasis of leisure for the father in the white ethnic neighbourhood who sits in his armchair surrounded by sons and sons-in-law, a beer within reach, watching the game on TV until mother serves dinner at 5.30 p.m. sharp. But California surfs and sails. San Francisco enjoys the scintillating reverberations of the evening sun over the Bay. On this Sunday we walked around, bought a balloon, looked at a man whose hat, jacket and bicycle were covered with strangely worded buttons; we stood between a Korean evangelist on Market Street and an angry man who interrupted the sermon with a stentorian voice saying: 'You are not an American,' and listened to a black woman who with an air of autistic happiness spoke to herself via a mike about Jesus.

Chicago was still on our minds. We had had some interesting discussions with community organizers. One of them told us that there are as many jobs available in the new corridors of high technology in O'Hare and Schaumburg as there are unemployed people on the South Side. Industries that hired masses of people in the last fifty years in the far South and in northwest Indiana have slowed down their production and are now nearly obsolete; but high tech is up and coming. So why don't the poor people move there? The answer is not so simple. They would have to be retrained. How else could someone become a key-punch operator? If we embarked on this task, would we also provide a chance for people to be humanly retooled as well and to rediscover what it means to be part of a community? Is it not time, in the maelstrom of economic changes, to emphasize values like compassion in a city of conflicts? Aren't times of economic change an opportunity to emphasize values other than competition, exclusion and the winner-loser dichotomy? Which other values? That you don't put down others as losers. That you look for support from others rather than trying to control them. That you humanize society. That you bridge gaps between people. That you find solutions to community problems which allow all parties to win. That you focus on positive signs and on the strengths in people and institutions rather than bringing out negative elements and weaknesses. That you stand with the oppressed, and share.

But throughout the day something about San Francisco's grace let us unwind. We wasted our time, happy about the interruption in our schedule. On the corner of Lombard and Hyde, looking at the beautiful homes, the other brother said that one day he would like to decorate a house, by himself, for himself. It was a little dream not likely to come true. There was, however, in our medley of fantasies about houses and homes some hidden complaint. The reason was that suddenly we had a hard time coping with our homelessness. We didn't have a house here, nothing permanent. There was no way to settle down in our own atmosphere. Other brothers were thousands of miles away, in New York and on a hill in France where our community is centred. Where is home for us while we travel? We sleep in other people's guestrooms. We live out of our suitcases. We are constantly underway listening, sharing, praying. Where is home for us?

But then, standing on the corner of Lombard and Hyde, overlooking the Bay, we had this moment of contemplation in which we repeated to ourselves that our home is Christ. We have no other home than where he leads us, no other home than where he meets us. He meets us with a balloon in his hand, with buttons on his hat, jacket and bicycle, he stands between an angry man and a Korean evangelist, he hums along with the ecstasy of a black woman. Home is where we see the sailboats dancing and the evening sun going down. Home is where we see a couple, reconciled, going to the video store to pick out a movie for tonight. Home is where we leave ourselves, suffer with the unemployed in Chicago and rejoice with the surfers in San Francisco. Home is wherever the Gospel comes alive. Home is where, at the end of the day, we decorate a little space with wax begonias and four-leaf clover, with candlelight and a cross. Home is where our love is. Love is the home Christ wants us to enter into, to be welcomed into, and . . . to decorate.

4

A Brief Tenderness in a Labyrinth of Longing

(The story of Bethlehem) does not exactly in the ordinary sense turn our minds to greatness. . . . It does not exactly work outwards, adventurously, to the wonders to be found at the ends of the earth. It is rather something that surprises us from behind, from the hidden and personal part of our being; like that which can sometimes take us off our guard in the pathos of small objects or the blind pieties of the poor. It is rather as if a man had found an inner room in the very heart of his own house, which he had never suspected; and seen a light from within. It is as if he found something at the back of his own heart that betrayed him into good. It is not made of what the world would call strong materials; or rather it is made of materials whose strength is in that winged levity with which they brush us and pass. It is all that is in us but a brief tenderness that is there made eternal.

G.K. Chesterton, The Everlasting Man

(1) The Road To Birth

> 'A woman giving birth to a child has pain because her time has come; but when her baby is born she forgets the anguish because of her joy that a child is born into the world. So with you: Now is your time of grief, but I will see you again and you will rejoice, and no one will take away your joy.'
>
> *John 16.21–22*

I once received a letter I have cherished ever since. Like the woman in the painting by Vermeer I sometimes take this letter in my hands to read it again, leaning on the sill of an open window or sitting at the table in the evening. Letters we like the most are printed in our hearts at the same time as we read them. We knew everything that is written down there. We didn't know that it would be written down, in this handwriting, on this day, in this way. But we don't need to read the letter again: its contents are part of ourselves. However, you want to read it again, to look at the stamp, to know where it was sent from, to follow the movements of the handwriting, to believe that this was written and that this was written to you.

So when I take up this letter I do so in order to be reminded of what I discovered in myself about the person who wrote the letter and about me who received the letter: that sudden light shed upon the far shore across the water, the far shore within ourselves; the amazement in discovering that from our footprints behind us the desert where we passed has blossomed, a fertile land carpeted with flowers; the opening of a road leading through life and darkness until dawn comes and the morning star rises in our hearts.

The person who wrote this letter was dying herself, and she wrote in order to console her correspondent in a time of bereavement:

'How can we understand that we march towards the Resurrection while going through such sorrowful events, through all kinds of suffering?

'For several months, because of my illness, I myself have been going through periods of suffering, and most of all I involve in my suffering those to whom I am linked.

'And nevertheless I see the last months as months of light: through this suffering that I experience and that I share with others, God has revealed to me his love by fulfilling me with the love of others. He gives always the strength to go through our suffering, he carries us taking our suffering upon himself, fulfilling us beyond obscurity, even in the midst of obscurity, by a fullness of joy and of jubilation before him.

'Come into his presence with songs of joy,' even if sometimes our voice is strangled, because the voice continues to sing although from time to time one doesn't hear its sounds anymore.

'Day after day I grow towards the very strong, existential certainty that it is not possible to see, and to go through death, one's own death or the death of another, as a sad event: sorrowful perhaps but *radiant* and joyful.

'I would like to share with you this sweet certainty, hoping that you and those around you will be filled with serene joy.'

(2) All The Living, All The Dead

> He looked at those seated in a circle around him and said, 'Here are my mother and my brothers! Whoever does God's will is my brother and sister and mother.'
>
> *Mark 3.34–35*

Church is at its best when it enables us to cross over into another world, the world of the Epiphany and the Resurrection at every litany and liturgy.

Chants resound in the freshly painted vaults as I enter an Eastern Orthodox church in Madison, Wisconsin. The church choir, which consists of as many nationalities as there are voices, is led by a university professor whose gestures mime invisible wings. The professor is a Serb, son of a Serbian Orthodox priest who left Austria-Hungary upon high school graduation because he didn't want to fight in Franz Joseph's army. In Kansas City, explains the professor, divided groups come together over his father's grave, when on Memorial Day they go around blessing the graves. The professor loves the Orthodox tradition as only one who has left it and returned can love it. How does a little boy explain to his elementary schoolteacher why he should be excused from school on 7 January because it is Serbian Christmas? As a beginning graduate student at Columbia University in New York, he literally wandered the streets at night, distraught, unshaven, bleary-eyed. He went to his priest and said: 'I no longer believe in any article of the Nicene Creed except the first, I still believe in God.' The priest's answer was: 'My dear, I know how it is but always remember the Church believes for you.'

In this small church in Madison the icons are still too

new to be true and the frescoes show Frankenstein faces of the celestial hierarchy. But the twinkling eyes of the university professor orchestrating his choir of angels, the opening and closing doors of the iconostasis, the myriad signs of the cross, the wavering lights of the candles and the Kyrie sung at regular intervals say that heaven and earth touch one another.

Church is at its best when it introduces us to the mystical communion of all the living and the dead.

I walked with friends through Augsburg, West Germany. In one of the old city's alleys the door of a convent stood open. Greek immigrants in Germany use the chapel every now and then. That day babies were being baptized. Mothers and fathers gave us signs to enter and to come closer. Sweet light rested in their dark eyes, radiating love for all those babies, anointed one after the other, signed with the cross on all parts of their smooth bodies, plunged from head to toe in the holy water of baptism. The priest sang in some strange tone cantabile passages. Ohs and ahs, applause as well, reverberated in the chapel. A video camera buzzed like a honey-bee while filming the embroidered baptism quilts. We stood on our toes, in pure wonder, looking beyond the shoulders of the Greek wanderers gathered on this island of consolation amidst the laments of death we carried with us from outside.

Church is at its best when it shows us, in the proud mothers presenting their babies to God, in the flickering eyes of the old standing in front of the candlestick like Simeon and Anna in the temple, the family we belong to, our mothers and brothers and sisters, with children in the middle.

(3) Wandering and Wondering

Mary treasured up all these things and pondered them in her heart.

Luke 2.19

A pilgrimage song (Psalm 84) says: 'They make their way from height to height.' Between height one and height two there can be some awkward moments. Pilgrims cannot constantly remain on a zenith, neither in their prayer and faith nor in their lives. But although they periodically have to descend from their heights, ultimately they make it. Serenity can become ours if we listen to God's call, again and again, amidst our experiences of unceasing failures. These failures we go through teach us what is essential in life and what is worth striving for so that we pray: 'My soul is thirsting for You. Your love is better than life itself. You have always helped me'. (Psalm 63). So we don't want to stay below; being pilgrims we search for whatever direction our yearning for God may take. We ask ourselves: What are the signs in my life which concretely indicate the direction I have to take? For whom should I live? Where can I find the face of Jesus in this city? What is the next step? Or: Should I go to the seminary? Should I take a year off, travel in order to find God's will? Do I risk changing my job for one which I believe will be more helpful to others? What should I do in order to centre my life on the Gospel more trustfully than before?

Those questions are hard to answer. In general we don't encounter overwhelming signs. Or are there very clear indications which we are not able to grasp because we are not simple, not single-minded enough? Should I go here or there? I am afraid of this, I want to be sure of that, I want this and I want that. Our difficulty is recognizing the sign. People challenged Jesus: 'What sign can you show us as authority for your action?'

At first the answer sounds almost eccentric: 'Destroy this temple, and in three days I will raise it again.' Three days? It had taken forty-six years to build the temple (John 2.19). The people who challenged Jesus didn't ask themselves what this could mean to him; they argued about it in their own terms.

Christianity is a way of learning to discern, a way of wisdom. When we are penetrated by what we have understood of the Gospel, when our mind, our feelings and our reactions are shaped by faith and prayer, we will know where the heart is, where the essence lies, in all things. How to grow in this discernment? By living the gift of faith, by being attentive enough in prayer to allow ourselves to be shaped, by listening carefully enough to those who are close to us so that we let them bend our will, by breathing the breath of the Spirit, by having that mind in us which was also in Christ Jesus (Philippians 2. 5). In *The Pilgrim God* Brother John of Taizé sees this as 'the deepest logic of the Bible': '. . . the light that radiates from God's face shines on the hard stone of the human heart and in the end transforms that stone into a mirror that reflects God's own image. This transformation, of course, does not take place in a strictly linear fashion, with no gaps or backsliding. And yet it never stops, like water that always makes its way, digging a channel through even the hardest rock.'

Mary often did not understand what was happening. But she treasured all things in her heart, surrounding them with love, filtering them with light until she entrusted them to life. Just keep your questions in mind. Keep them open toward faith, keep waiting for an opening of the Gospel in you. Just keep them, until a ray of light begins to spread its light in your inner room.

(4) The Hundredth Sheep

> 'When he finds it, he joyfully puts it on his shoulders and goes home. Then he calls his friends and neighbours together and says, "Rejoice with me; I have found my lost sheep."'
>
> *Luke 15.5–6*

Why did the hundredth sheep go his own way? Why did the sinner go astray? How can I find a way to join the flock again and return to the shepherd?

My fear of feeling denied, my anguish at being deserted – having been myself swaddled as a small child by motherly love – paradoxically leads me, propels me into a contemplative attitude of welcome. Precisely there where I am tempted to repulse others when they touch critical zones of my being, I discover the incentive for a contemplative tenderness with regard to them.

My 'collaborators' are this insecurity in facing others and this continual dependence on others. These collaborators make it possible for me to exist harmoniously instead of being driven by the anxiety of being dropped or excluded. Intentionally isolating oneself can be a form of possessively making claims on others.

For me the danger lies in the tendency to cut myself off from others, keeping others at a distance, out of the fear of being wounded by the very closeness I long for. This is a defence mechanism. What comes from others has first to be screened, before I can welcome whatever others want to convey to me. I have first to overcome the trauma of a possible rejection. I would remain very much isolated in my feelings if there were not the mystical dimension that allows me not to dry up in this isolation. This dimension reaches out to the far shore of myself and opens a way to others that lies between affectionate exuberance and the introduction of a defensive screen.

I could instinctively refuse the community with others or keep myself at a distance because of the fear of being made dependent on others or the fear of losing the sympathy of others. In which case, in order not to victimize others, there would be no other solution than to oscillate between an attitude of irony and some acrobatic way of giving myself, between a pseudo-free isolation and the fixation on others. Also, my capacity to trust weakens when I register the signals given by others – signals which are perhaps, in reality, neutral – as wounding or as a rejection.

I have to go through, again and again, this fear which inhabits me, invades me or immobilizes me so that an inner harmony can be woven between what others offer and my welcome of it. Is it not in this combat, in the solitude of this crossing over that I am clothed with Christ?

Praying with and watching over others in their serene dance through life – nearby or faraway – is my task. This watching is for me a way of seeing the face of others disentangled from my fear. In this way I live in the dimension of gratitude, which in turn protects me against the invasion of fear and everything that comes with it: aggressiveness, disappointment, feelings of failure, tiredness caused by isolation, possessiveness. And I discover that in order to live, and to bring to life, I cannot not celebrate others and watch with tenderness over them, in the hiddenness of the other's life and of my own life. Even if, because of the invasion of fears, the gift of my person or the investment I make in a relationship is limited to this little space of celebration of others – there where I am in consonance with Christ – even if this little space is sometimes pushed away to the periphery of my existence, or even if there remains only the bare desire to celebrate – I rejoice!

Definitely, I am the hundredth sheep.

(5) Here at Horizon's Crossroads

'Everyone will be salted with fire. Salt is good, but if it loses its saltiness, how can you make it salty again? Have salt in yourselves, and be at peace with each other.'

Mark 9.49–50

Faith becomes mouldy if we don't nourish ourselves with the bread of our innermost life. Faith smoulders and dies out if we don't set our existence on fire. Faith becomes a routine and fades away, if we don't let it reach the heart of life. If we don't 'do the truth' with the faith that we have received as a gift, faith becomes a theological scrabble, a game of playing with words or a romantic sublimation of the abysses that terrify us or even a lofty alibi for power manoeuvres. Faith reduced to some sociological attitude turns us into masterminds obsessed by programmes, doings and happenings or pseudo-martyrs crusading against the world's amoralism. We become statues of salt. We reinstate rituals with a glass of sherry in the left hand, debating with elegance which chasubles are the simplest. We cease to touch that depth of the Gospel which reverses culture and sophistication, wealth and scepticism, power and haughtiness. We forget about Jesus' violence and mystical love of God, restraining ourselves to some selected passages of Jesus' moral teachings because they have been recognized by the world's standards of respectable values. We exclude the lower classes from our celebrations, and instead of becoming signs of contradiction we see the role of the church as enabling us to meet the notables of our town and gown, gathering together as the chosen few against the dark forces outside the country club.

A perceptive Episcopal priest on the West Coast showed me pictures of a church celebration in Africa, and exclaimed: 'I look at all those African bishops and wonder why they accept being such a transplant of the Church of England. That is an aspect of the cross of our tradition: we don't want to lose our privileges and become symbols of contradiction by taking and reversing our upper-class mentality and going into the depths.' He himself has tried to be ruthless with his church because of the need to go to the bottom of things, to the source. In the seminary his classmates told him, 'Don't think so much, don't ask questions, you are going to disturb things, just let it go.' And yet these are the people he now finds looking for something substantial, having lived through a disavowed agnosticism, not knowing where to find faith.

We need a living faith. How can we sustain our faith beyond its initial awakening? Often we are good at beginnings, but how can we go beyond that? How can we enter into a discerning process so as to bring out the gifts still inert in us? We hear the invitation 'Come up higher' but we believe that obviously we have not been built for

the Gospel. At a certain moment we have to choose and
to go beyond stage one. At a critical time – and from that
moment on again and again – standing at the crossroads,
a choice has to be made.

I walked into a house of contemplation in Raleigh,
N.C. where some women live among poor blacks. While
one of the women was making coffee for the guests, I read
on the wall the framed rules of this Madonna House:

'Arise – go! Sell all you possess . . . Follow Me – going
to the poor – being poor – being one with them – one
with Me.

'Little – be always little . . . simple – poor – childlike.

'Be hidden. . . . Go without fears into the depth of
people's hearts . . . I shall be with you. I will be your
rest.'

These calligraphed simple words on a wall in North
Carolina reveal to me that faith means losing oneself.
Our choice need not be directed to extra things to be
done, but to lose and to lose again, to lose ourselves in
God. Faith is not a success story, for anybody. We are
not built to live the Gospel. Even Jesus said that only
God is good. No good can come out of our own strength.
It is hard to embody the Gospel. The only way I have
found to remain attentive to the radical nature of the
Gospel has been to commit myself for life to live, together
with others, a parable of community. Faith involves us in
an ongoing experience of community; through a community we belong to a people; in community we follow
the living Christ. In a monastic community in particular,
the structures of life have no other finality than to lead to
the Gospel. Is community, in whatever degree, not the
only way for us all to help ourselves to radiate something
of the Gospel in our own life?

Someday we will have to choose, someday there will

no longer be time to lose. Someday we won't be able to protect ourselves any longer. It will be 'yes' or 'no.' Because faith is a question of life or death.

(6) Before The Silver Cord Gives Way

> Jesus was in the stern, sleeping on a cushion.
>
> *Mark 4.38*

When with the coming of evening you are asleep in the stern sheets of the ship, I behold you, between the hither and the farther shore.

Your head rests on a cushion, streaked like a shutter of fibrous wood in the sunset, veneered with gold leaf, closed on the house of your dreams. A halo adorns your face. A blanket of camel hair lies spread about you, wrapped round, incandescent in a bed of embers. Waves rock you as though in a cradle, from shore to shore. Don't you hear the stooping gulls wishing to conceal you with their pinions? Don't you hear the cross-tree pine and yearn? Don't you hear the sail catch the wind? And the din of voiceless cries?

I crouch next to you beholding you asleep. Were you so tired? All this talking and arguing, all these crowds and compulsions have tired you so that you want to sleep out in the sunset. You sleep like a child – dreaming in the balance of the waves, breathing between two ripples, seesawing toward the far shore of longing.

I sit on my heels at your feet and look at the sails and the horizon and the firmament who all witness you. With the coming of evening I rest in the presence of a child whose face rests in the arms of sleep. I rest as a leaf whirling in the air, as a cloud on its sacred procession through the sky. I rest in your rest. I yield myself to you in your sleep. As a weaned child on its mother's breast my soul is at peace. I wait but all I am waiting for is with me.

You know the long storm that rushes through my life, you know the chaff, the rock, the thistles, you know the labyrinth in which I run, the places of wailing and grinding of teeth, you see me walking and waking to escape an indefinable threat. Where is home? Here where you are asleep, here where I rest in you.

You are asleep in me, as a child breathing life. You are asleep in my heart as its waves beat the inner shore. When will you rise? The thundercloud, the cold rains, the fury of the wind are coming. When will you rise?

Before the silver cord gives way, and the golden lamp falls apart – give me the gift to give myself to you as you rise from the sleep of death. Give me the gift to give myself to you as you rebuke the long storm, and warn off the monsters of the labyrinth. Give me the gift to give myself to you who walk with me along an inner shore, from solitude to solitude.

And when the silver cord gives way, when I will fall asleep forever, give me the gift to rest, give me the gift to rise in you.

(7) Roots and Blossoms

> 'I am in my Father, and you are in me and I am
> in you.'

John 14.20

By reversing the Lord's prayer new dimensions open up, bringing new life to our daily recitation. Starting with the most common human experience of evil, we go through the storms and turmoil of our existence, until we finally lift our eyes towards God. Plunging through turbulent rapids and following steep descents we return to the still source of God. Like the prodigal son who once dissipated himself on the wrong side of town and tottered in a whirlpool of tears, we come home, welcomed in the arms of our Father.

Pausing after each demand, personal prayers welled up in me. But each person is invited to add his or her personal intentions to my list of prayers. These intentions could be followed by a Kyrie eleison, either spoken or sung.

> *Deliver us from evil*
> from rushing
> from dying alone
> from abusing trust
> from hoarding our gifts
> from destroying ourselves
> from hardening our hearts
> from having no thirst for justice
>
> *Lead us not into temptation*
> of resting upon our own strength
> of depending on visible results
> of losing the key of knowledge

of taking the easy way out
of retreating from others
of settling down
of betraying

As we forgive those who trespass against us
who destroy
who abandon us
who refuse to forgive us
who minimize our vocation
who separate and divide us
who tell us a truth too hard
who extinguish the life of the Church

Forgive us our trespasses
for hurting others without realizing it
for being afraid of people's suffering
for fearing other people's judgement
for harbouring negative attitudes
for excluding those who don't love us
for excluding ourselves
for eluding you

Give us this day our daily bread
give us silent joy
give us a flair for forgiving
give us the gift to give ourselves
give us the pleasure to rejoice in others
give us eyes to see your love in the morning
give us living water in the desert of our days
give us the grace to lose ourselves in you

Thy will be done on earth as it is in heaven
your will is like a creator seeing that his work is
    good

your will is like sunlight breaking through the mist
your will is like a valley full of bones brought to life
  again
your will is like a morning star we long for in the
  night
your will is like a plough cutting furrows in our
  hearts of stone
your will is like our parents' voices as they prayed
  aloud
your will is like a newborn child in times of
  bereavement

Thy Kingdom come
let the fields exult and all the rivers clap their
  hands
let the nations come running up to embrace each
  other
let us be born again from the womb of the Spirit
let lambs and wolves go aboard the ark together
let the mustard-seed sprout in our hearts
let us see you in a breeze of wonder
let us open the door when you knock

Hallowed be Thy name
our God is good
our God is eternity
our God is a devouring fire
our God is the heart of every heart
our God is unspeakable love
our God is Spirit
our God is God

Our Father who art in heaven
our Father
Father

(8) Born To Be Born

'Before Abraham was born, I am.'
John 8.58

Is it babbling or glossolalia when we speak the words
that stand aligned on the oscilloscope of our unconscious-
ness? 'Before Abraham was born, I am,' said Jesus. I
know no other words as capable of turning my logic
upside down and of leading me down beneath voluntary
structures and controlled security into the dimension of
the heart.

You woke me at the oak while I was asleep, tired from
the long road to birth. I had wanted to be ready; as a
matter of fact, I had been – on the eve, and again at
midnight, at early dawn also. But you came so unex-
pectedly. I had been sitting there for a long time, at first
hoping, waiting and longing for you but then I fell into a
light sleep. However, it was good that you could come
and that you woke me. You must have stood there quite
a while, at the zenith of the day. Only when I heard you
whispering did I wake up. You whispered: 'Sleeper,
awake.' It sounded like the voice of my mother. How
long ago did I hear that voice! Was that sound so deeply
rooted in me, so hidden underneath every other sound
that you alone could awaken it? Your whisper went
through all the layers of life back to a moment of
unspeakable happiness when I heard for the first time
the voice of love.

At first I hadn't seen who you were. I only saw a light
breaking through opaque walls. Only gradually I
understood that you had arrived, at a time I least
expected you. I lifted my eyes to you. You had woken
me, and now you shaded me. With you before me, the

119

sun could not strike me down by day. Your visit was grace. I didn't want to detain you and I knew that you had to go elsewhere, further. Further before earth came to birth, before mountains were born, before anything was. Only when I saw you shading me did I awake. You gave me the seal of the Promise. Good hands received me, like those of my father. How long ago had I felt the shape of his hand! Was this vibration so deeply sensed in me, so hidden underneath every other experience that you alone could reveal it? You have always been there through the stages of my life back to a moment of unlimited belonging when for the first time I found the warmth of love.

Before? Before mountains were born, before earth came to birth, before anything was – in a mother's womb, in the good hands of a father – born to be born.

(9) God Has The Eyes Of Those We Love

> 'If your right eye causes you to sin, gouge it out and throw it away.'
>
> *Matthew 5.29*

One evening we had set one hour apart to meet as brothers among ourselves, before evening prayer. One of us had gathered some texts, mainly from the Church Fathers, about the theme of the beauty of God.

Our eyes can find no rest, no refreshment in a city like New York. Too many images, especially the stark or ugly ones, devour our peace of mind. Images of rundown buildings, images of litter on the stoop, images of neon-lit pubs, images of fearful eyes, images of prostitution, images of human degeneracy, images in ourselves awakened by what we furtively glance at, images that shock or wound or obsess. It is easy to get overwhelmed, contaminated, even corrupted in the city. It is a temptation not to draw out of ourselves creative images, not to uncover in ourselves healing images with which we would face the evil so present in the space between the images of the world and the worldly images in ourselves. Is it possible to work, inside ourselves, on a way of looking that would convey joy, courage, faith, solidarity? More than words, our eyes say everything about ourselves and about others. Our entire vocation, our entire ministry, the ministry of the whole Church depend on the way we look at others.

To give our eyes rest, and to create in ourselves a new way of looking we need art, simple furniture in our apartment, times of silence (we don't speak after evening prayer until morning prayer the next day), love among ourselves. We need above all to rest in God. 'Is it conceivable,' I ask the brothers 'to imagine God with human features and to borrow the eyes of those we love in order to represent God? Is it reasonable to think that we find in God all the love we received from our parents, from friends, from people who have linked their lives to ours? I can't imagine anything more beautiful than the expressions on the faces of those I love. And I see all these expressions in God, the source of Love. It seems to me that one day when it is time to close our eyes, and open them again in God's closeness, we will see all the love we have received, given and longed for in our life. All that love is ahead of us, and therefore we can be looking forward to that hour in which we will close our eyes.'

The brothers understand. They see that I want to let the experience of longing and love flow into their very

source in God. But they add also that God is beyond
every experience and longing and love, 'way beyond.'
God is the source of light, 'light of light.' Who would
know the beauty of God?

(10) Letter For a Baptism

> 'I am the good shepherd; I know my sheep and
> my sheep know me – just as God knows me and
> I know God – and I lay down my life for the
> sheep.'
>
> *John 10.14–15*

My own baptism took place one week after my birth. In
spite of the harsh winter I was rushed to church. For my
parents it was the first thing to do. A child is a gift of
God. This immediate reflex of my parents has been a
reference for me throughout my life and has inspired my
own decisions.

Next Sunday a niece and a nephew, sixteen and
seventeen years old, will be baptized. Better late than
never! It is an opportunity for me to rediscover the
implications of my own baptism. So I write them a few
words:

The fact that I can't be there is not so terrible. So often
I feel that absence does not exclude a real presence. If
there is a celebration, one wants of course to be together;
there can still be in our existence a deep attitude of
festival and celebration in spite of mutual absence and an
apparent inaccessibility of the other.

If this is true for our whole life, it is even more true for
an event like your baptism. By being baptized you are

given entry to the reality of the communion in Christ, in which each one carries the other and where you are upheld by eagles' wings as long as you yourself sustain the uplifted arms of others. In your baptism that communion becomes your horizon.

Are you acquainted with that drawing by Paul Klee: a proliferation of little sailboats etched together with one single line? Each little boat is part of the whole flotilla. Did you ever see, at sea or on a lake, the dance of bobbing sailboats, one beyond the next, advancing in a wide circle, with shifting shadings around them, under the shimmering sun reflecting itself on the water surface? Through baptism your voyage becomes dependent on the voyage of the others. With each of them you are invited henceforth to create a space of communion within, with the visible and the invisible, knowing that because of you their history becomes a procession towards Christ. Through baptism you are not alone any more. Rather, you are invited to believe that in every encounter and in every commitment the others will be present and will accompany you until one day the measure of all love will be fulfilled.

All the people with whom you will be together this coming Sunday are a sign of the large circle of those who, although invisible, surround you, are a sign of the communion of the Church. I hope this Sunday will be a day of joy because you enter a mystery which is the secret of our lives and the source of happiness, even if we, young or old, can't grasp this completely, a mystery that the risen Lord one day will disclose to us in all its meaning and coherence.

(11) Becoming Like Children

> He called a little child and had him stand among them. And he said: 'I tell you the truth, unless you change and become like little children, you will never enter the kingdom of heaven.'
>
> *Matthew 18.2–3*

Does faith imply a personal, conscious, mature knowledge, as I was told in my youth around the time of confirmation? Should one become a semi-theologian in order to believe? Should faith be appropriated as a philosophy after having weighed its probabilities and scrutinized its plausibilities? In my youth theologians were still venerated heirs of the truth who possessed an exclusive right to revelation and who, from their high pulpits, dropped magisterial credos down like confetti on a submissive crowd. I used to sit on the highest steps of the staircase leading to the pulpit in the overcrowded church of my youth, listening to them.

But then the crisis came. At home we discussed on Sundays and on weekdays if the serpent in Eden was a myth, if Luke had written the letter to the Hebrews, if the resurrection was an oriental tale. Suddenly there was a suspicion among older people that they had been deceived over a period of fifty years. They said: Why did the theologians not tell us of their doubts? Why didn't they say that our faith was not so certain after all? We had learned everything about predestination, pre-existence and post-millenarianism. As students we discussed, while drinking loads of gin, if it was morally permissible to dance the foxtrot. On Sunday we listened to sermons asking if Jesus had ever smiled or laughed.

And now we stood in the world, either as stubborn fundamentalists affirming that if the facts would contradict us, so much the worse for the facts, or as frustrated freewheelers flirting with any extemporaneous thought that happened by.

But what about all those people not capable of grasping hairbreadth nuances? What about ourselves on the day we will be cut off, in a flash, from logical schemes of thought? What about the handicapped? What about the singing faces of the mentally disturbed I saw in Ottawa gathered together for prayer and song? Oliver Sacks, the neurologist, recently told the story of one of his patients who was totally without memory. He admits having considered him a 'lost soul,' as a man 'de-souled' by the disease. What about him? 'Do you think he *has* a soul?' the neurologist asked the Sisters in the Home for the Aged where the patient stayed. '"Watch Jimmie in chapel," they said, "and judge for yourself." . . . I watched him pray, I watched him at Mass, I watched him kneel and take the Sacrament on his tongue, and could not doubt the fullness and totality of Communion, the perfect alignment of his spirit with the spirit of the Mass. . . . Clearly Jim found himself, found continuity and reality, in the absoluteness of spiritual attention and act.'

What we need in order to believe is a spiritual intelligence, the intelligence of the poor. Above all, we need to need faith. We need to need Jesus' hand stretched towards us. And we need to walk on water in order to need that hand. We need the one thing necessary, and we need to need that one thing by becoming aware of our poverty. A Jesuit told me long ago that I was a very good soil for the victory of faith. I must have communicated a lot of doubts. Doubts immobilize, and you still want to win against your deepest self where you have received the gift of faith. In doubting you postpone your commitment, and commitment is precisely the preamble of faith. In doubting you forget to praise, and praise is precisely the premise of faith. In doubting you lessen your love, and love is precisely the vehicle of faith. Let go of your urge to master faith. Become like Jesus in the temple, in the house of his 'Father.'

You knew it was true. You knew, you've always known, that nobody but Jesus has the words of eternal life. Stand up for it. Turn round, and become like a child.

(12) In Mother's Arms (A Psalm Prayer)

> A woman in the crowd called out, 'Blessed is the mother who gave you birth and nursed you.' He replied, 'Blessed rather are those who hear the word of God and obey it.'
>
> *Luke 11.27–28*

Many people yearn for silence. But how to fill it up when it is finally there? Silence can be empty, silence can be violent. In silence we can dream away or fall asleep. Inner storms wait for silence and then they burst out. A concrete idea for starting a time of silence is to write a prayer using the words of psalms. It can lead to inner silence, especially when one finds there the words that express our innermost thoughts. With inner silence we can approach in peace whatever proceeds from our heart. In inner silence we dwell in Christ, our peace.

I wrote down this psalm prayer:

'My sighing is no secret to You,
My heart is full of fear,
I stay awake, lamenting as a lone bird on the roof,
I say, "Oh for the wings of a dove to fly away and
to find rest."
Why must I walk so mournfully, oppressed by the
enemy?

Let my cry for help reach You,
Let your face smile on Your servant,
Let me wake in the morning filled with Your love,
Put into me a new and constant spirit,
Will you not give me life again?

You tested me, God,
You refined me like silver,
You let me fall into the net,
But now the ordeal by fire and water is over,
And you allow me once more to draw breath.

You pull me out of the slough of the marsh,
You give breath, fresh life begins,
By your light I see the light,
I will walk in the land of the living,
You made me, and I belong to You.

God, I have trusted You since my youth,
I have relied on You since I was born,
Placed on Your lap from my birth,
From my mother's womb You have been my God
Enough for me to keep my soul tranquil and quiet

Like a child in its mother's arms.'

(13) 'The Virgin Sings Her Lullaby'

'I tell you the truth, unless one is born again,
one cannot see the kingdom of God.'

John 3.3

Flannery O'Connor's illness prevented her for several weeks from sleeping. She was aching to go to sleep. In a letter to a friend she wrote: 'Since then I have come to think of sleep as metaphorically connected with the mother of God. Hopkins said she was the air we breathe, but I have come to realize her most in the gift of going to sleep. Life without her would be equivalent to me to life without sleep and as she contained Christ for a time, she seems to contain our life in sleep for a time so that we are able to wake up in peace.' After reading this passage, I began to think about Mary singing, as in the Greensleeves Carol: 'What child is this, who, laid at rest, on Mary's lap is sleeping . . . Raise, raise the song on high, The virgin sings her lullaby; Joy, joy, for Christ is born, the babe, the son of Mary!' It surprised me that I dared to think of her in such a way.

In my Calvinist tradition Mary was taboo, however strange that may sound. It was strictly forbidden to pray to Mary because of the possible competition with Jesus and of the potential confusion between the humanness of Mary and the divinity of Christ. Mary was even lower than the disciples. The theology of 'the Mother of God' seemed an extreme heresy. One of the results was a very stubborn religion, terribly tense concerning Christ's uniqueness. Its reason was the total incommunicability between the natural and supernatural worlds, crossed only once and for all in Christ. We therefore had only fathers and forefathers in faith, no mothers; we became efficient and hard-working, very alert and constantly preoccupied Christians, more convinced of God's punitive justice than of God's reconciling love, more pervaded by the fear of condemnation than by the spirit of childhood. We were unable to sleep in the stern amidst the storms of the world; we couldn't see our existence as one long Christmas night. Would we have believed in Christ's birth in us today?

It is so easy and natural to venerate Mary, the mother of Jesus. She is the air we breathe. She prays with us. She contains our life. She is our Mother and we see her in every mother. I saw her in the woman I met after an evening worship in Grand Rapids, Michigan. This woman told me that every evening she sings with her children before they go to sleep. They repeat one song over and over again, together like a chant. And when the children fall asleep, she still sings.

Mary was present in my own mother who used to sing me to sleep. Now she is asleep in God's arms. And I sing to her.

(14) A Brief Tenderness in a Labyrinth of Longing

> 'I am God's servant,' Mary answered. 'May it be to me as you have said.' Then the angel left her.
>
> *Luke 1.38*

In transparence
a crenellated light

In silhouette
Aeolian sails

Parting
for the other fruit of the days

Index of Gospel references

(adapted from the *New International Version*) (New York: New York International Bible Society, 1978).

Footnotes

Section 1

Edwin Muir, 'The Transfiguration' in *Collected Poems*, New York (Oxford University Press), 1965, p. 174.

(1) About the Shakers, see *The Shakers. Two Centuries of Spiritual Reflection*, edited by Robley Edward Whitson, New York (Paulist Press, The Classics of Western Spirituality), 1983.

(2) *Collected Poems*, o.c., p. 139.

(10) The music of 'We Rely On The Power of God,' written by Richard Hillert, is published by GIA Publications, Chicago, 1983. The Shaker songs are quoted in *The Shakers*, o.c., pp. 294–295, except the second one 'I have come to sweep.' This one can be found in: Edward Deming Andrews and Faith Andrews, *Fruit of the Shaker Tree of Life*. Memoirs of fifty years of collecting and research. Stockbridge, MA. (The Berkshire Traveller Press), 1975, p. 174.

(13) This definition of monasticism partly depends on Isaac of Stella, Sermo 12, Ed. J.P. Migne, *Patrologia Latina*, vol. 194, Paris 1855, c. 1731 B.

(14) A friend who read this meditation wrote in the margin this poem of E E Cummings: 'Seeker of truth / Follow no path / All paths lead / Where / Truth is here.' Dietrich Bonhoeffer speaks in *Letters and Papers from Prison*, London (SCM Press), 1973, p. 376 of a 'beyond' which is 'not what is infinitely remote but what is nearest at hand.'

Section 2

Hymn sung in the 1866 'Mercersburg Liturgy' of the German Reformed Church in Pennsylvania (now part of the United Church of Christ).

(2) Shusako Endo, *Silence*, New York (Taplinger Publishing Co.), 1979, pp. 258–259.
'Be quite undone and never more be done,' see Edwin Muir, 'The Transfiguration,' see footnote at I.

(14)   In preparing this sermon I was inspired by G.K.
       Chesterton, *The Everlasting Man*, New York (Dodd,
       Mead and Company), 1930, which I had read on the
       plane from San Francisco to Omaha.

Section 3

Thomas R. Kelly. *A Testament of Devotion*, New York
(Harper and Row), 1941, pp. 83–84.

(10)   Enrique Dussel. *Philosophy of Liberation*, Maryknoll, NY
       (Orbis), 1985.
(11)   Richard F. Lovelace. *Dynamics of Spiritual Life. An
       Evangelical Theology of Renewal*, Downers Grove, Ill.
       (Inter-Varsity Press), 1979, p. 336.
(13)   Thomas Merton. *Conjectures of a Guilty Bystander*, New
       York (Doubleday), 1968, p. 21.

Section 4

G.K. Chesterton, *The Everlasting Man*, o.c., pp. 222–223.

(3)   Brother John of Taizé, *The Pilgrim God. A Biblical Journey*,
       Washington, DC (The Pastoral Press), 1985, pp. 211–
       212.
(7)   For the melody of 'Kyrie eleison,' see *Music from Taizé*,
       London (Collins) and Chicago (GIA).
(11)   Oliver Sacks, 'The Lost Mariner,' *The New York Review of
       Books*, February 16, 1984, pp. 14–18.
(12)   Psalm verses 38.9; 143.4; 102.7; 55.6; 43.2; 102.1; 31.16;
       90.14; 51.10; 85.6; 66.10–12; 40.2; 104.30; 36.9; 116.9;
       100.4; 71.6; 22.10; 131.2.
(13)   'The Virgin Sings Her Lullaby': Hymn 40 in *Lutheran
       Book of Worship*, Minneapolis (Augsburg), 1978.
       Letter to 'A,' October 20, 1955 in: Letters of Flannery
       O' Connor, *The Habit of Being*, selected and edited by
       Sally Fitzgerald, New York (Farrar, Strauss, Giroux),
       1979, p. 112.